# *12* Steps
## To A More Effective Christian Witness

*Alvin Velsvaag*

TATE PUBLISHING, LLC

"Twelve Steps to a More Effective Christian Witness" by Alvin Velsvaag

Copyright © 2005 by Alvin Velsvaag. All rights reserved.

Published in the United States of America
by Tate Publishing, LLC
127 East Trade Center Terrace
Mustang, OK 73064
(888) 361-9473

Book design copyright © 2005 by Tate Publishing, LLC. All rights reserved.

No part of this publication may be reproduced, stored in a retrieval system or transmitted in any way by any means, electronic, mechanical, photocopy, recording or otherwise without the prior permission of the author except as provided by USA copyright law.

Scripture quotations marked "MES" are taken from *The Message Remix*, Copyright © 2003. Used by permission of NavPress Publishing Group.

Scripture quotations marked "NIV" are taken from the *Holy Bible, New International Version* ®, Copyright © 1973, 1978, 1984 by International Bible Society. Used by permission of Zondervan Publishing House. All rights reserved.

ISBN: 1-59886-07-5-5

## Dedication

There are literally billions of people in this world that suffer from one thing or another. Some of the big causes of this suffering are addiction, abuse and mental illness. Many of these people are in your own back yard. Our neighbors in pain are exactly who God is asking us to reach out to; we need to tell them that God is the great source of hope, power and compassion that will lead them through their difficulties. My prayer is that this book will help you do just that. With this hope in mind, I dedicate this book to "those who still suffer."

# Acknowledgments

The first acknowledgement I must make is to the loving God that I met as a child, drifted away from as a teen and who today is my constant companion, the God to whom I owe everything and the God that has so richly blessed my life with miracle recoveries and wonderful friends.

I must also acknowledge the many twelve step groups, such as Alcoholics Anonymous, that I have had the privilege of being associated with over the years. They have been so important because that is where I developed my deep faith in and dependence on the loving and compassionate grace of God. Through this process I have met too many people to mention. They have had profound effects on my recovery; you know who you are, thank you.

I do however have a bit of a problem with acknowledging my affiliation with Alcoholics Anonymous because of their eleventh tradition stressing the importance of personal anonymity at a public level, yet it is virtually impossible to talk about the twelve steps without mentioning Alcoholics Anonymous. Allow me to begin addressing this concern by saying I in no way, shape or form speak for Alcoholics Anonymous and am in no way a representative of Alcoholics Anonymous. I have the deepest respect for them and their traditions. I am not even claiming to be a member of Alcoholics Anonymous at this time in my life. I do however believe a weekly twelve step commitment is important in recovery; I attend a Christian twelve step group at my church.

    I have struggled with how to handle this and considered using a pen name, but decided to go ahead and use my real name because I believe it is vitally important to have an open discussion about addiction, abuse and mental illness in our society today and I believe the best way I can help this happen is by setting a good example. Using my real name demonstrates that it is okay to talk about these matters publicly. I have peace with this decision and hope the wonderful people of AA will understand why I feel it is so important, especially in the context of mental illness, to use my full name.

# Table of Contents

1. Why Reach Out to Others? . . . . . . . . . . . . . 13
2. Who Do We Reach Out To? . . . . . . . . . . . 33
3. Can They Be Reached? . . . . . . . . . . . . . . . 41
4. Do They Want Help? . . . . . . . . . . . . . . . . 49
5. My Experience Strength and Hope . . . . . . . 57
6. Steps and Prayers . . . . . . . . . . . . . . . . . . 71
7. The Twelve Step Community . . . . . . . . . . 87
8. Twelve Step History . . . . . . . . . . . . . . . . 95
9. We Need to Understand Powerlessness . . . . . 103
10. We Must See Our Own Need First . . . . . . . 111
11. Trust God . . . . . . . . . . . . . . . . . . . . . . 119
12. Clean House . . . . . . . . . . . . . . . . . . . . 129
13. Give and Receive Forgiveness . . . . . . . . . 141
14. Help Others . . . . . . . . . . . . . . . . . . . . 153
15. Attract Others to Christ . . . . . . . . . . . . . 163
16. Some People Fear the Church . . . . . . . . . 171
17. Feeling Judged . . . . . . . . . . . . . . . . . . 183
18. Is Our Absolute Truth Theirs? . . . . . . . . . 199
19. Effective Help is Ongoing Help . . . . . . . . 213
20. Will We Always Make a Difference? . . . . . 221
21. We Love Who God Puts in Front of Us . . . . 229
22. Why do Bad Things Happen to Good People? . 233

## Foreword

You've just picked up something very special. Alvin Velsvaag's life may be different than most. It is marked by years of addiction, abuse, mental illness, recovery, and a strong faith in Jesus Christ. Alvin clearly understands his purpose in life and how God has shaped him to fulfill that very special purpose.

As you read this book you will soon realize Alvin's perspective is unique and can only come from someone who has walked the addiction pathway, lived a life with the struggles of mental illness issues and abuse, and now walks the road of recovery. Alvin's knowledge of the twelve steps of Alcoholics Anonymous and his clear understanding of God's hand in his life shine through on every page.

This is a passionate book written by someone who believes in the awesome power of God to transform lives and the incredible tool available in the twelve steps. If you or someone you know is struggling with addictions, abuse, or mental illness issues, this book will increase your understanding. If you have been involved in twelve step programs, this book will help you gain a greater understanding of just whom your higher power truly is. And for you folks who have had little experience with addictions, abuse, and mental illness, this book will certainly be a real eye opener. You will come away better equipped to understand and help those who are still suffering.

Alvin has told me he wouldn't trade his life for anything and feels he remains on this earth to help others in their struggles and to try and teach those not afflicted to gain a better understanding of those who are.

It's a pleasure for me to recommend this book and I thank God for Alvin and the message of encouragement and understanding he shares. It's a blessing that God has crossed our paths and honor to call Alvin my friend.

Scott Pederson
Pastor of The Journey Church
Nisswa, MN

# Introduction

The purpose of this book is to help people better understand the relationship between the twelve steps of Alcoholics Anonymous and the Bible. It is written to long time Christians that have little or no experience with some of the darker sides of life such as addiction, abuse and mental illness, in the hope that they will be able to gain more understanding of the twelve step way of life and learn how they can be a witness to, and of service to those who still suffer.

It is also a very good resource for anyone that has a family member or friend caught up in these dark behaviors. By reading this book you will add to your understanding of them, yourself and of the twelve step process that has helped so many people find their way through such great difficulties.

The third group of people that will benefit greatly from this book are those that have been in a twelve step program and are searching for a better understanding of God, as they understand Him. I believe this book will help you greatly in seeing the relationship between the twelve steps and the Bible.

I have always been of the opinion that there is too big of a gap between the twelve step community and the Christian church. By learning more about each other that gap can begin to close. As you read on, you will learn of the great need that exists in our society today for people willing to reach out with a helpful, compassionate hand; you will learn more about the people that need this help and then, in chapter five you will meet me.

The next section of the book introduces you to the twelve steps and takes you through them so that you may gain a better understanding of yourself, your journey with God and your relationship with others. If you are familiar with the Bible and not so familiar with the twelve steps you will be amazed at how the twelve steps are basically just good Christian living.

The last chapters of the book are dedicated to improving your witness to those who still suffer. It contains some do's and don'ts of witnessing to people that are living lifestyles that lead to pain and suffering. It will explore how both you and they think, which will promote understanding and decrease any fear you may have by letting you know more of what to expect when you reach out to others. Every time one person is reached for Jesus, the angels rejoice; you will find it to be a wonderful and rewarding experience when you rejoice with them.

# 1. Why Reach Out to Others?

Oftentimes in conversation about all the pain and suffering in this world, the following question has come up. Why, if God loves us so much, and heaven is so wonderful, does He leave us here in this fallen world instead of whisking us right off to heaven the moment we are saved? Although there are many reasons that God may have, that our finite minds may never grasp, there is one reason we can easily see. He left us here for the benefit of others, especially for the benefit of those who still suffer.

Christians often speak of "Christ likeness"—the process of maturing spiritually where we gradually become more like Christ. Jesus was many things in His years here on this earth, some of which we will never become. He was perfect and sinless; no human other than Him can ever achieve this. Also, He was and is the Savior of all mankind, the Messiah, another unachievable goal for humans. However, sometimes we seem to think we can be someone's savior, a situation that in my experience only seems to get in the way of the real savior and tends to perpetuate trouble instead of solving it (codependency).

Christ is a terrific teacher and a tremendous example setter. Qualities to some extent, we can emulate. We will never be "perfect" at it, but we can continue to try to do a better job today than we did yesterday. To borrow a phrase from AA (Alcoholics

Anonymous), we claim spiritual progress, rather than spiritual perfection. One of the biggest examples Jesus set in His time as a human here on earth, was that of reaching out to people in great pain. He paid a lot of attention to the sick, the lame, people tormented by demons, the poor, the helpless, the downtrodden and the outcasts. This is a category people suffering from addiction, abuse and mental illness most certainly fall into. We don't need to look very far to find such unfortunate people; they are all around us. The Bible says:

> "Keep on loving each other as brothers. Do not forget to entertain strangers, for by so doing some people have entertained angels without knowing it. Remember those in prison as if you were their fellow prisoners, and those who are mistreated as if you yourselves were suffering."
> (Hebrews 13:1–3 NIV)

> "For I was hungry and you gave me something to eat, I was thirsty and you gave me something to drink, I was a stranger and you invited me in, I needed cloths and you clothed me, I was sick and you looked after me, I was in prison and you came to visit me. . . . The King will reply, I tell you the truth, whatever you did for the least of these brothers of mine, you did for me."
> (Matthew 25:35–36, 40 NIV)

It is obvious that the Bible instructs us to reach out to those who suffer, yet often we don't think much about these Biblical suggestions because we get so caught up in our own lives. The Bible talks a lot about thinking of and helping others, instead of being self-centered. Being self-centered is the state that comes naturally to us humans and is exactly where "sin" would like to keep us. The great paradox is, the most selfish thing we can ever do is to give of ourselves to others, especially to people whose lives are cloaked in the darkness of addiction, abuse or mental illness.

Matthew 6:20 speaks of storing up treasures in heaven. Often this passage is refereed to in messages about giving money to the church. Certainly, the money we have contributed to God's kingdom here on earth will have its rewards in heaven. Some people would also say that any kindness done toward another here on earth stores up treasures in heaven. Near the end of the movie "Ghost" the character played by Patrick Swazi, who has been a ghost trapped here on earth for a while, makes a profound statement as his spirit is finally about to ascend to heaven. In essence he says you get to take the love you feel in this life with you to heaven. The old saying, "you can't take it with you" most certainly applies to money, but does not apply to the loving way we have treated others.

According to Rick Warren, "We bring God glory by telling others about Him" (The Purpose Driven Life" page 57). As you read on you will find that running up to someone and proclaiming Jesus as the risen lord and savior is not always the best way to start reaching out to someone. Eventually however, introducing them to the awesome healing power of Jesus Christ is the goal. This is a point that needs to be developed in greater detail and will be later in the book. It is sometimes hard to hold back your excitement and enthusiasm for Christ, yet sometimes this overbearing approach can push people further away.

The truth is, the most exciting thing that will ever happen in your life will be when God allows you to be part of the miracle He is working in someone's life. Make no mistake about it. Jesus is still a miracle worker and heals people from their pain and suffering everyday. People whom society has branded as "hopeless" are rescued from the depths of addiction, abuse, depression, and mental illness on a regular basis. Through my involvement in twelve step groups, I have had the great privilege and honor to witness and to be part of many such miracles. I have also been the recipient of such a great miracle. It is with absolutely no hesitation or doubt that I share with you, were it not for the all-powerful, unending grace of God, I would be institutionalized, insane or dead, instead of sharing the message of how much God wants to use you in the healing of suffering people.

People that have had long term involvement in twelve step groups such as AA become spoiled by the number of miracles they have witnessed and can sometimes be disappointed with the lesser number of such miracles witnessed in the Christian church.

This is true in part to the fact that God often uses someone who has been through a particular hurt to help heal another person with that same hurt. This is a very good thing and this concept in the working of miracles will never be replaced. You do not however, have to have suffered the same or similar darkness to become part of the miracle in someone's life.

If people in the Christian church would take some time to better understand the types of people that are having miracles performed in their lives in twelve step groups, they would be better able and equipped to reach out and welcome these people into the Christian church. Getting into a good church home is oftentimes nearer the end of these miracles than the beginning. It is none the less an extremely important part of the miracle. By bringing more of these miracles into the Christian church, the Christian church would become an even more exciting and rewarding place to be.

Don't feel bad about not understanding twelve step groups and the people in them very well. You are in good company. In the Saddleback Church in California, the church that Rick Warren is the senior pastor of, they have developed a Christian recovery program called "Celebrate Recovery." They are helping some people with their hurts, habits and hang-ups and have made the materials available for other churches. This is a very good thing; anytime someone from the church reaches out to those in need, the angels rejoice. They are, however, a prime example of how twelve step groups such as AA are misunderstood by people in the Christian church.

On the Celebrate Recovery website (www.celebraterecovery.com), Rick Warren included an article titled "Message by Pastor Rick." In it he displayed an obvious lack of understanding of AA and other twelve step groups. He said he had always been uncomfortable about the vagueness of God in AA and then proceeded to lay out seven things that made Celebrate Recovery unique among recovery groups. I was disappointed to find someone of such notoriety spreading false information about twelve step groups. This disappointment produced the following letter to Rick Warren:

---

Dear Pastor Warren;

Hi, my name is Alvin and I am a recovering addict/alcoholic. I have great respect for your work and have read "The Purpose Driven Life" along with much of the "Celebrate Recovery" material. Thank you for seeking God's call on your life and I pray that you continue to seek His guidance. The subject of this letter is to address the way you seem to perceive AA and the way that you misrepresent it in your "Message by Pastor Rick" on the Celebrate Recovery web site. Before continuing, I must make it perfectly clear that I do not represent AA and the following is my understanding of AA, based on the exposure I have had to the twelve steps of AA over the past twenty-six years. I also want to say upfront, I don't believe you intentionally misrepresent AA, apparently you don't really understand AA.

I received Christ as my savior at the age of accountability and grew up a regular attendee of a Christian church that did a good job of teaching me the Bible. However, the person that pushed going to church the most, is also the person that hurt me the most and this hypocrisy pushed me away from the church. Realizing I had an out of control drug and alcohol problem, I started attending AA. They encouraged me to seek God and turn my life over to Him, yet this was difficult because of my bad experiences with "Christian people." My struggle continued for the next 16 years and I was unable to achieve sobriety. Now, thanks to the absolute healing power of God, I have ten years of continuous sobriety. This relationship with God and His son Jesus Christ has been strengthened and supported more by AA than by the Christian church. I have tried many times in my adult life to feel as if I belonged in a Christian church, but it was to no avail.

Again, thanks to the awesome grace of God, a year ago I found a recovery friendly Christian church where I have been welcomed and feel comfortable. I can't tell you how wonderful it is to have "come home"!!! This small E-Free church has a heart for reaching out to the un-churched in the community. Almost immediately the pastor and I began having discussions about recovery and how large the twelve step community is in our area. Many of these people do not have church homes, but have been introduced to God in groups such as AA. It is our mutual feeling that these groups are doing a good job of pointing people, some with a great aversion to the Christian church, in the direction of God. What we see missing is the hand of the Christian church, welcoming these people into a safe place where they can explore a personal relationship with Jesus Christ and gain a better knowledge of the Bible, without being pushed. Our intention would never be to replace the twelve step community, but to equip our church to build on the foundation started with so many people in AA.

My pastor had been to a Celebrate Recovery meeting at Saddleback and has great enthusiasm about starting a group in our church, but was never able to find someone to really commit to it until God brought Pastor Scott's desire to reach out to those who still suffer along side my desire to promote more understanding of twelve step programs and the people in them to the Christian community. At first glance, it seemed impossible for our small church to get such a thing going; it appeared too complicated with all of its different components. We decided to go forward in the simplest way possible and started a weekly meeting to go through the twenty-five topics in the Celebrate Recovery workbooks. We actually have more people from the church without major problems in their lives than we have recovering people. We think this is what God wants for now, so these well meaning and committed Christians can learn more about recovery and themselves, better equipping them to welcome people that are really struggling into our church.

In true alcoholic form, the group had been going for nine months before I decided to go to the internet and research Celebrate Recovery. I was excited to find a representative in my state, but came away from a conversation with him feeling hurt and disappointed. Apparently, the effort we have made is not good enough to be recognized as a Celebrate Recovery group and our conversation pointed out some differences of opinion. Number one of these concerns was his negative attitude towards AA. I was further disappointed to find that both your message and John Baker's testimony seem to contain a negative feeling about AA.

You spoke of the "vagueness of the nature of God" in AA. In the opening of every AA meeting I have ever attended, the first two and a half pages of chapter five out of the "Big Book" of Alcoholics Anonymous has been read. In this brief reading, God is directly mentioned or referred to fourteen times. The last two statements read are "That probably no human power could have relieved our alcoholism" and "That God could and would if He were sought" (Alcoholics Anonymous, page 60). To me, there is nothing vague about that at all; in fact, I would call it very direct. AA is not vague about the nature of Jesus Christ either; they simple do not speak of Him by design. They say nothing good or bad, specific our vague, Christ simply is not the topic. As for the "Holy Spirit," I have never sensed His presence stronger than I have in AA. The Holy Spirit started and guides AA in much the same way He started and guides your church. If you doubt that, read about Bill Wilson's (cofounder of AA and author of the twelve steps) conversion experience (pages 120 and 121 of "Pass It On, the Story of Bill Wilson and how the AA Message Reached the World"). It was every bit as dramatic as that of the apostle Paul.

Most of your "seven features that make it unique" are not unique to Celebrate Recovery. I know that you would not intentionally bear false witness against anyone or any group of people. The problem with doing it unintentionally, even though it may be due to a lack of understanding, is that many people wondering if Jesus Christ could be their personal "Higher Power," may read this on your website, realize at a glance that it is untrue, and consider you and by extension, the entire Christian church, hypocritical. This of course could turn that person away, making a person that was at one time looking to Christ more difficult to reach for Christ in the future. The following are comments about each of your "seven features that make it unique."

Unique feature number one: "This program is based on God's word, the Bible."

To imply that yours is the only recovery program based on the Bible seems a little arrogant, again, a quality that would tend to push many people away from Christianity, instead of attracting them to it. AA is absolutely and firmly based on the Bible. Not only did they use the beatitudes as a road map, they used the entire Sermon on the Mount, the thirteenth chapter of first Corinthians, and the book of

James. Please consider the following excerpt from page 147 of "Pass It On":

"Bill now joined Bob and Anne in the Oxford Group practice of having morning guidance sessions together, with Anne reading from the Bible. Reading . . . from her chair in the corner, she would softly conclude, 'faith without works is dead.' As Dr. Bob described it, 'They were convinced that the answer to our problem was in the Good Book. To some of us older ones, the parts we found absolutely essential were the Sermon on the Mount, the thirteenth chapter of first Corinthians, and the Book of James.' The Book of James was considered so important, in fact, that some early members even suggested "the James Club" as a name for the fellowship."

Unique feature number two: "This recovery program is forward looking. Rather than wallowing in the past, or dredging up and rehearsing painful memories over and over, Celebrate Recovery focuses on the future."

AA greatly emphasizes harnessing the power of God to start making better choices for today and the future. You are partly correct though; AA also believes in examining one's past in order to make peace with it (Steps 4 through 9). They also believe that having a basic understanding of their own past, makes AA members much more useful to God in helping others deal with their hurts, habits and hang-ups. Please examine the following quote from the "Big Book" of Alcoholics Anonymous, which comes directly after explaining steps 1 through 9 to the reader. This section is commonly referred to as "the promises" and is somewhat longer than this quote.

"If we are painstaking about this phase of our development, we will be amazed before we are half way through. We are going to know a new freedom and a new happiness. We will not regret the past nor wish to shut the door on it. We will comprehend the word serenity and we will know peace. No matter how far down the scale we have gone, we will see how our experience can benefit others." (Alcoholics anonymous, pages 83–84)

Unique feature number three: "This recovery program emphasizes personal responsibility."

The twelve steps of AA are completely about personal responsibility. They emphasize being responsible for your own understanding of, and relationship to God. Secondly, AA encourages people to take their own moral inventory, confess their wrongs, and then make restitution and amends. (AA also compels people to look at their good and positive qualities in this same process.) The last steps encourage people to take immediate responsibility for their current wrongs, to take responsibility for continued growth in their relationship with God, resulting in a spiritual awakening which instills a desire to reach out to others and in doing so, find their own "purpose driven life."

Unique feature number four: "This recovery program emphasized spiritual commitment to Jesus Christ."

Check out "Alcoholics Victorious," they

emphasize the same. I have also attended a group called "Twelve Steps in Christ" that fits this description. As far as AA goes, just because they do not endorse Jesus Christ, does not mean that they oppose Him. They have very carefully and purposely made the decision to leave God, defined as, "God, as we understood Him." There are millions of people that suffer from grave ailments such as alcoholism that would simply never go somewhere they thought they would be evangelized, and if they did, and salvation through Jesus Christ were pushed on them, they may never come back. Just the word "God" as it is often used in AA, is enough to make such people cringe, yet as they get use to it, they become more ready to hear the wonderful message of salvation through Christ. This is however never the purpose of an AA meeting; it can't be, or AA would become too exclusive and their goal is to reach out to absolutely everyone that suffers from alcoholism.

This does not mean that many people do not hear the message of Jesus in one-on-one conversation before and after meetings, they do, but first they must see something desirable in the person that is witnessing for Christ, or why would they want to hear this message from them. This "something desirable" in a Christian is often noticed at meetings by non-Christians and causes them to seek out the Christian for further discussion of their "Higher Power" after the meeting.

I was disappointed in John Baker's testimony. (John Baker is an associate pastor at Saddleback and is the person that developed Celebrate Recovery.) After sharing that 90 AA meetings in 90 days saved him from the depths of alcoholism, his last word about AA was negative and left a gross misconception about AA. AA does not mock anyone's understanding of God, including that of Jesus Christ; they rejoice in the fact that someone has realized they are not God. That is not to say that someone's faith won't be ridiculed by certain individuals in AA, it will, especially if someone crosses the line into evangelism in an AA meeting. Again, AA is not against evangelism, an AA meeting is just not the appropriate place for it. This sort of evangelism in an inappropriate place can appear to non-Christians as a lack of respect for the traditions of the group and push people further away from Christ.

John's testimony also leaves an impression of running away from being identified as a believer in Christ. Doesn't Christ ask us to stand firm in the face of such criticism? I know for myself, such experiences have presented opportunities away from the meeting to talk with such individuals more specifically about my understanding of God. After all, isn't that what Jesus would want me to do, instead of never coming back because my feelings were hurt? (Before I start sounding too self-righteous, allow me to interject the fact that I also have difficulty returning to a place where my feelings have been hurt, that is why I have had such a hard time returning to the Christian church. I am greatly comforted by the AA principle of claiming spiritual progress, rather than spiritual perfection.)

Unique feature number five: "This recovery program utilizes the Biblical truth that we need each other in order to grow spiritually and emotionally."

AA is absolutely "built around small group interaction and the fellowship of a caring community." This is the very essence of AA, the very core principle upon which it was established, a principle they picked up from their intense study of the book of James. There is also, however, plenty of room for "one-on-one interaction." (Pastor Warren seems to discount the importance of one-on-one interaction in his letter.) AA would never presume they could help with all of someone's problems and discourage them from seeking professional one-on-one help from doctors, psychiatrists, counselors, psychologists or pastors. In fact, AA often advocates taking advantage of these tools that God has made available to us and has always attempted to be respectful of and friendly with such professionals. Another vitally important one-on-one relationship that goes to the core of AA is sponsorship, a place where many AA members do come to Christ. Isn't the accountability partnering that is so often recommended by the Christian church "one-on-one interaction"?

Unique feature number six: "This program addresses all types of habits, hurts and hang-ups."

Yes, AA has adopted an attitude called "singleness of purpose." They exist solely to help anyone who has a desire to stop drinking, stop drinking, and they do it well. They have, however, made all the literature and steps available for adaptation to any problem people are having. It is also important to say that any hurt, habit or hang-up a person in AA is having, that threatens their peace of mind, and therefore their sobriety, is fair game for discussion at a meeting. If you take the twelve steps as they were originally published in the "Big Book" of Alcoholics Anonymous, and replace the word "alcohol" in the first step, with the word "sin," the twelve steps of AA become an umbrella under which the entire human race can fit.

Unique feature number seven: "Finally, this recovery program produces lay ministers!"

Everyone in AA is encouraged to find a way they can be of service. This may be as simple as emptying an ash tray, but it is service. The vast majority of people that stay sober in AA are successful because they have learned to give back what had been so freely given to them. This giving back takes many forms, all of which I would have to consider "lay ministries."

My first hope in writing this letter is that it will further educate you on what AA is really all about, so that you, like many other pastors and professionals, can become a friend of AA. AA deeply respects and invites the cooperation of people that have reached the prominence and stature in their field that you have, and would be the first to say, to God be the glory for your accomplishment. I believe, with further consideration, you will see that we are all on the same team; that in the end, we share the common goal of reaching out to those who still suffer.

Secondly, I would like to further define the vision we have for the Celebrate Recovery meeting at our church. The main objective is to bring the local twelve step recovery community and the Christian church community closer together, to bridge the gap that I have always perceived to be too wide. It is my belief that this gap exists more from lack of understanding, (on both sides) than for any other reason. This is why we rejoice at the opportunity to go through the four Celebrate Recovery workbooks with people that have been long time members of the Christian church, without such dark problems in their past. One reason is so they can deepen their own relationship with God, themselves and others, through the self examination encouraged by the twelve steps. The second is so they might gain a better understanding of people that are caught up in such dark lifestyles, so it is easier to be empathetic and compassionate to those who still suffer and help them feel more welcome and at home in our church.

Our extended hope is that we will begin, as a friend of the twelve step community, to draw in some of the twelve step people who would like to trace the origins of the twelve steps back to the Bible, a job that is so well accomplished by the topics, Bible readings and questions contained in the Celebrate Recovery workbooks. We are in no way anti-AA; in fact we wish to be supportive friends of AA, as well as with the many other twelve step groups in our community. We have no desire of replacing them, only a desire to pick up where they leave off, leading people in need to Christ.

In order to bridge this gap between communities, the Christian church needs to start building a bridge on the foundation of understanding, from their side. As much as I enjoy the opportunity to work with my fellow recovering addict/alcoholics, I am certain that God is calling me to carry this message to the greater Christian community, especially those that have belonged to the church for most of their lives and have had no direct experience with addiction, abuse, or mental illness, promoting this much needed understanding of those who still suffer. I am convinced that our churches contain many such people who are very well meaning and have a great desire and willingness to reach out to people in such darkness, yet lack a basic understanding of said darkness and are therefore afraid to move forward. Also, I believe there are some of these well intentioned Christians that are moving forward without a good understanding, and at times inadvertently pushing people further away from Christ. Wouldn't it be great if we could mobilize this great army of "Christian soldiers" into effective action and lead many thousands more of the people who suffer greatly, to the awesome healing power of our Lord and Master Jesus Christ?

Thank you so much for taking the time to read this letter. I will be prayerfully anticipating your response. Please feel free to contact me at any time.

Sincerely;
Alvin Velsvaag

## Why Reach Out to Others?

Won't you decide right now to become a part of bridging the gap between the secular twelve step community and the Christian church? It will be one of the most rewarding journeys you have ever embarked upon. You can become part of this process by deciding to learn more about the twelve steps and in the process you will learn more about yourself. I know that many of you have a deep desire and willingness to serve the Lord in this way, but you are unsure of how to go about it. Helping you with this issue is the purpose of this book.

The Christian church must begin to build this bridge from their side, on the foundation of understanding. By learning more about yourselves through the twelve step process and more about those that are attracted to the secular twelve step community, you will have less fear and apprehension in reaching out to those who still suffer. With less fear and more knowledge, you will become a more effective witness for Christ.

One last reason for the people in the Christian community to reach out to the secular twelve step community is this. Whether we build the bridge or not, others will. AA and similar groups use a generic God, leaving the interpretation of God open to each individual. This is a very good thing, because it makes these groups very inclusive; no one is left out. This is a little hard to understand and will be explained in greater depth later. When you have this type of environment, many different ways of interpreting

God will show up. I will promise you, whether the Christian church befriends the secular twelve step community or not, other groups of thought, such as New Age, will be there.

Some of these New Age concepts are very deceptive. They often use some Christian language and even speak of Jesus and refer in part to the Bible. They speak a lot about love, relationships and getting along. They also seem to be infatuated with angels. Many people are drawn down this path thinking they are learning more about Christianity. There are, however, some troubling differences. They have other texts beside the Bible such as "A Course in Miracles." They believe this to be as much the word of Jesus as the Bible is. They believe that we (Humans) are co-creators with God, that God comes from within us, we are the miracle workers and their seems to be a complete lack of belief in Satan, a place he loves to be, for one of his favorite tactics is to blend in, to be invisible, to have you believe he is not even there. This makes his work much easier.

Twelve step groups such as AA do a very good job of pointing people towards God. It is the job of the Christian church and those in it to be sure and be there to offer the understanding of God that is presented in the Bible. This can be done by forming a cooperative friendship with the generic twelve step groups. A respectful friendship on behalf of the Christian church, that is ready to pick up where the twelve step community leaves off in defining God. This is your job!

## 2. Who Do We Reach Out To?

One doesn't need to look far to find people experiencing pain and suffering. Drug and alcohol abuse, victims of childhood sexual abuse and people with mental illness are all around us. Many of these people at sometime end up in twelve step programs and often all of these problems can be found in one person; they seem to go hand in hand. People with these problems are also common in our churches; some of these people never speak of them because they are afraid of harsh judgment or exile from others. They feel like no one will care or can help and they are convinced that no one else has ever felt as bad as they do. Just how common are these hurts? The following statistics speak for themselves.

According to the NCADD (National Counsel on Alcoholism and Drug Dependence), about eighteen million Americans are problem drinkers and there are five to six million Americans with drug problems. To put these numbers in perspective, over half of the adults in America have a history of problem drinking in their family. Over nine million American children are growing up with a parent dependent on alcohol and /or illicit drugs.

Stop Child Sexual Abuse (www.stopcsa.org) estimates that somewhere between one out of three and one out of four women and between one out of seven and one out of eight men have been sexually abused by the time they are eighteen.

NAMI (www.nami.org) reports somewhere between five and ten million adults and three to five million children in the United States have serious and disabling mental illness. Of course many millions more have less than disabling mental illness, yet it is enough to still create challenges and issues in their lives.

Drug and/or alcohol addiction and sexual abuse need little defining, most everyone has an idea of what they entail, but mental illness is often a different story. Many people cannot name the major mental illnesses and when picturing it they think of "crazy people" suffering from schizophrenia or something like it. Schizophrenia is of course one of the mental illnesses and causes major disruption in the lives of those who have it. There is an abnormality in their brain which makes it difficult to distinguish between what is real and what is imagined. This makes up a very small percentage of the mentally ill.

Some of the common mental illnesses are: bipolar disorder, where the affected person will be on tremendous highs, sometimes going without sleeping for days, and then crash into an extremely deep depression. Obsessive compulsive disorder is sometimes characterized by obsessive hand washing and cleaning or carefully followed rituals. With panic disorder, the person's system produces too much adrenaline which in the long run makes them very fatigued, and it is sometimes accompanied by agoraphobia, causing the person to have difficulty leaving home. Post dramatic stress disorder, made known by Vietnam veterans, is in no way limited to war. It often develops in victims of abuse and can manifest in different ways. Hallucinations are common, and some of these hallucinations can involve all five senses. Attention deficit disorder is another common mental illness that has an early onset and often affects children; it can cause problems for the person's entire life. There are others but these are some of the common ones.

Most of these people are not crazy and their illness is not always visible. When a person is disabled by one of these illnesses, it can be harder than having a more visible handicap, such as being confined to a wheel chair. When a disability can't be readily seen, people don't seem to accept it as well and expect the disabled person to be able to do more than they are capable of.

Unfortunately, this is only part of the suffering that is prevalent in our society today. When you add in other hurts like spousal abuse, addiction to other things like gambling and sex, and let's not forget the pain of divorce, you can see it is not hard to find someone who suffers to whom we can reach out to in the name of Christ.

It is so vitally important that the Christian church does all they can do to understand and welcome these individuals. The love of Jesus and a welcoming, caring, compassionate church family can go a long way in helping to ease the great pain such unfortunate people feel.

We must, however, realize that no one source of help can be the total treatment such people need. Oftentimes twelve step groups or caring churches, although they help immensely, are not enough. We must encourage those that suffer from some of these grave ailments to seek professional help as well. God has given us many tools to deal with these conditions: psychiatrists, psychologists, counselors, support groups and treatment centers to name a few. One big thing Christian people can do is help lessen the stigma that has been attached to using such resources by assuring people that it is not only all right to make use of them, but in fact is very wise; that reaching out for help is not a sign of weakness, but a source of strength.

People have not chosen to have these conditions; for the most part, they were born into these situations. Life situations of this nature do not indicate moral weakness or inferiority, for the most part they indicate illnesses and disorders that are every bit as much an illness as cancer or sugar diabetes. Situations they cannot heal from without outside help. They are powerless over them, a topic we will cover at great length as you read on.

It is so vitally important for all of us in the Christian community to think about another phrase commonly heard in AA. "But for the grace of God go I!" Any one of us could have been born into a family situation that produces sexual abuse, or could have been born with a genetic predisposition to mental illness or into an environment that breeds alcoholism.

We all have imperfections and weaknesses, but we also have many good things going for us and we need to be very thankful to God for all that we have; it is all a gift, a gift that at anytime could be lost. Think about the book of Job in the Bible. Job had many riches for which he was grateful and lost all but his life very quickly.

A more recent example would be that of Christopher Reeve. He was on top of the world with money, fame and a brilliant acting career when in a split second while riding a horse he lost nearly everything he held dear. I would guess that he, like most people, took the ability to walk and care for himself for granted. We need to realize that because our life seems to be going better than that of others, we aren't better than those who still suffer, we are just more blessed. A blessing that were it not for the grace of God could disappear in a heartbeat.

Unfortunately, many of us have someone close to us, a spouse, relative or friend that fits into this broad category of hurting people. Maybe this is your motivation for reading this book. It is very good to gain a better understanding of the problems our loved ones face. Perhaps some of you fit into the codependent category, someone that has been greatly affected by the darkness in the life of a person close to you. Oftentimes, people in this codependent type of relationship are so focused on the problems their loved one is having, they are not aware of the tremendous hurts that have built up in themselves. Alanon and other groups like it are very helpful in healing the hurts of the codependent. It is always amazing to hear the story of someone that has come through one of these damaging relationships; frequently, they make the person with the primary problem look sane.

People often ask what they can do for their loved ones who are caught up in addiction and the like. The first thing you can do is pray for them and keep praying for them. This not only focuses God's attention in their direction, it will help you to better let go of the situation so you are not so affected by it. Secondly, educate yourself about the problem your loved one is having. This will help lessen your fear and also help you to know what to be supportive of in their behavior and what behavior to not support. The serenity prayer that is so often used in the recovery community encourages us to change what we can, accept what we can't change and to seek the wisdom to know the difference. Other people always fall into the category of things I cannot change, and my own example is something, with the help of God, I can change.

Your example is one of the most powerful witnessing tools you have. Set an example that says it's OK to reach out for help by reaching out for help yourself. Set an example that it's good to learn about the challenges we face by learning about them yourself. Set an example that its good to stare denial in the face and own up to your problems by being rigorously honest about yourself, with yourself, and finally set an example that God can and will help by turning your own life over to the care of God. When you take control of your life back from God, as we all inevitably do, turn it over again, and again, and again. You truly can find peace in your life, whether this important person in your life is getting help or not, and nothing is more attractive to someone in turmoil than seeing the kind of peace of mind that God offers, in you. They may actually ask you someday where you get such peace from and what a great opportunity that will be to witness for Christ.

Oftentimes in twelve step groups, situations arise where a spouse or family member has tried to help an alcoholic for years. They have all but given up when all of the sudden some stranger comes into the life of this hurting person and seems to be able to help when the loved one has failed all these years. The natural human tendency is for this person to become jealous or even angry that they couldn't help and this stranger came along and could. This is very common, but maybe it was the loved ones continued prayers that urged God to send this stranger into the life of the alcoholic at just the right time. This concept of oftentimes not being able to help those closest to us is illustrated in the Bible when Jesus says:

> *"But Jesus said to them, 'Only in his hometown and in his own house is a prophet without honor.'"*
> *(Matthew 13:57 NIV)*

Never loose hope as long as a person is still alive. No matter how far down they have gone, remember,

Jesus does still work miracles. Unfortunately, while hoping for this miracle, many people have to protect themselves and their children from being further hurt by the person that has gone so far down. You can still hope and pray from a safe distance. If the situation you are in with a suffering person causes a physical threat to you or your children, leave. Maybe things will work out later. This person may begin to heal, and it will be safe to return. You must also however prepare yourself for the possibility that this person will not get better; unfortunately, many of those who still suffer never do get better. In this sad circumstance, the people around this suffering person can get better and know peace, if they are willing to look at themselves and trust God with their own lives.

## 3. Can They Be Reached?

The numbers of people hurting and the many different ways they hurt can seem overwhelming, like an impossible task. How would we ever be able to reach all those who suffer, or even a significant number of them? Actually, reaching one of them is a significant number. There is an old story often told about a little girl running down a beach covered with thousands of starfish stranded by the outgoing tide. She was busily picking them up and returning them to the water. When a passerby asked why she was wasting her time when she couldn't possibly throw enough back to make a difference, she held up a star fish for him to see and as she threw it back into the sea. She said, "I made a difference for that one."

Growing up on a farm, my family was often confronted with what appeared to be impossible tasks. Sometimes we had to pick rocks off of a field covered by tens of thousands of rocks. Other times the task would be to stack a mountain of hundreds of hay bales. At first glance it truly did seem impossible, but we soon learned that by picking up the first one and going on to the next, and the next, with some perseverance, the job would get done. We did it one rock and one hay bale at a time. We also learned that if we never started the job, progress was slow. Another lesson learned was that two or three people made more progress than one. Yes the number of people hurting is great, but the number of people in the Christian church is great as well. The more Christians that join in the task, the more people they can reach for God. Ministry is not the job of the minister. It is a job that falls on everyone that knows Jesus. There are great numbers of other organizations helping disadvantaged people every day and certainly much is already being done from within the Christian church. It would however be a good thing if more Christians took the time to educate and equip themselves, so they can become a more effective part of this effort to reach suffering people.

The most important part of being able to reach people in need is that you believe even if they cannot be completely healed, their quality of life can be greatly improved. You cannot project hope if you don't believe there is hope. This is a good time to examine your own faith in the healing power of Jesus Christ. Have you entrusted problems and hurts in your life to God? Do you have experiences where with hindsight you can see how strongly God moved on your behalf? We all need God; yet turning our lives and our wills over to Him is a difficult thing. The first step in reaching out to others is to give your own life more completely to God. You may ask, "How can I do a better job of turning my life over to the care of God?" This is a question best answered by taking a closer look at the twelve steps. They will be covered in detail as you read on. Remember how important our example is. If the hurting person does not see something desirable in us, why would they listen?

You can also increase your amount of hope and faith that God does still work miracles by listening to the testimonies of people that have had dramatic recoveries. One place to find such testimonies is at an open AA speaker meeting. When AA directories are published in newspapers and the like, they are described in different ways. A closed AA meeting is only for people that have a desire to stop their problem drinking. An open AA meeting is open to anyone that is recovering from alcohol abuse as well as anyone that just wants to learn more about alcoholism. At the start of these open meetings, introductions go around the room, most people say "I'm (their first name) and I am an alcoholic." It can feel awkward when it comes to your turn and you are not an alcoholic. People in this situation just say their first name and leave it at that or say something like "I'm (Their first name) and I just wanted to learn more about alcoholism." Sometimes you will see AA meetings listed as open speaker meetings. This means that someone will get up and tell their story and a round of introductions is not made. Many non-alcoholics come to these meetings just to listen. That can be a good place to see and hear how actively God moves in the lives of people that make an effort to turn their lives over to Him, thereby increasing the amount of hope you have to project to others.

When I speak of miracles and healing I am not referring to faith healers that put on a big show and claim that a touch of their hand can make the blind see and the lame walk. These shows tend to arouse a little skepticism in many of us. Nor am I advocating praying and trusting God without doing anything else. God has given us many professionals to help us with our physical, mental, emotional and spiritual problems. These people are not the miracle workers, but they do become part of the miracle. The orchestration of the miracles referred to will always come from God. Usually though, he has enlisted a large cast made up of doctors, counselors, physiologists, pastors, caring Christian church members and people in support groups like AA.

Some examples of such miracles would be when a falling down drunk, whom society and even the medical profession has given up on, all of the sudden has the compulsion to drink taken away. Or when a girl that has been terribly abused finds the ability to forgive her attacker, starts loving herself and then is able to reach out and love others. Or when a person with severe panic disorder and agoraphobia is able to get up in front of people and share his love for God. These are just as much a miracle as the blind suddenly seeing, and they happen every day. Sometimes God comes to these people in a dramatic way, but usually it is more gradually. The common denominator is that these people have exhausted every means they could think of to rid themselves of the awful pain they carried, and in desperation, cried out to God for help.

There is no way to describe the feeling you get when you are allowed to witness and to be a part of such healing. People can be helped and there is hope.

The more you see and here of such miracles, the more effective you will be at projecting the kind of hope that brings them about. One of the best examples of God coming quickly to a person that was down for the count and society thought sure to be near the end, is that of Bill Wilson, cofounder of Alcoholics Anonymous. He had always been an intelligent and motivated person that did well at whatever he set his mind to. He had a loving wife and a brilliant career on Wall Street. Apparently though, he had never given much thought to God and he had known the pain of a broken family and the loss of someone close.

As his life went on, he began drinking more and more. It started to make his life unmanageable and cost him some important business relationships, but one of the deepest effects it had on him was how much his drinking was hurting his wife, Lois. He decided to quit and vowed to his wife never to drink again, but the compulsion to drink would get the best of him and he would have another bottle in his hands. He lost everything and couldn't hold a job. He ended up drying out on the drunk ward in a hospital many times. He had lost all hope when one day an old drinking friend showed up sober, telling Bill he had found religion and no longer needed to drink. Bill was skeptical at best. He didn't know what to think of this God stuff, but his old friend was sober. It wasn't long before Bill had gotten so bad again that once more, he ended up in the hospital drying out, a place he had been far too many times. His doctor, who had at one time held out hope for Bill, was giving a pretty grim prognosis. What happened next is best described in the following excerpt from "Pass It On, the story of Bill Wilson and how the AA message reached the world."

"Now, he and Lois were waiting for the end. Now, there was nothing ahead but death or madness. This was the finish, the jumping-off place. 'The terrifying darkness had become complete.' Bill said. 'In agony of spirit, I again thought of the cancer of alcoholism which now had consumed me in mind and spirit, and soon the body." The abyss gaped before him.

In his helplessness and desperation, Bill cried out, 'I'll do anything, anything at all!' He had reached the point of total, utter deflation—a state of complete, absolute surrender. With neither faith nor hope, he cried, 'If there be a God, let Him show Himself!'

What happened next was electric. 'Suddenly, my room blazed with an indescribably white light. I was seized with an ecstasy beyond description. Every joy I had ever known was pale by comparison. The light, the ecstasy—I was conscious of nothing else for a time.

Then, seen in my minds eye, there was a mountain. I stood upon its summit, where a great wind blew. A wind not of air, but of spirit. In great, clean strength, it blew right through me. Then came the blazing thought "You are a free man." I know not at all how long I remained in this state, but finally the light and the ecstasy subsided. I again saw the wall of my room. As I became more quiet, a great peace stole over me, and this was accompanied by a sensation difficult to describe. I became acutely conscious of a presence which seemed like a veritable sea of living spirit. I lay on the shores of a new world. 'This,' I thought, "must be the great reality. The God of the preachers."

"Savoring my new world, I remained in this state for a long time. I seemed to be possessed by the absolute, and the curious conviction deepened that no matter how wrong things seemed to be, there could be no question of the ultimate rightness of God's universe. For the first time, I felt that I really belonged. I knew that I was loved and could love in return. I thanked my God, who had given me a glimpse of His absolute self. Even though a pilgrim on an uncertain highway, I need be concerned no more, for I had glimpsed the great beyond.'

Bill Wilson had just had his 39th birthday, and he still had half his life ahead of him. He always said that after that experience, he never again doubted the existence of God. He never took another drink." (Pass It On, pages 120–121)

## 4. Do They Want Help?

Yes, people do want help, but often they don't know they want help. Every person is born with a need and a longing for God. It is as if we have some sort of hole or emptiness inside of us and we try to fill it with all sorts of things. Things like alcohol, drugs, food, sex, unhealthy relationships, work, gambling, material possessions, the list is endless. We, as Christians, know the only thing that fills this hole is the love of Jesus. Even when we do know Jesus, we can forget and fall back on filling the hole with things from the list. When we do, and the anxiety begins to return, we know it is time to look back toward Jesus and once again give our lives to Him. Isn't it wonderful there is no limit on the number of times Jesus will welcome us back and reward our coming back with peace of mind and soul?

The trouble is people that don't know Jesus can't really imagine that any such belief could really make much difference. This again is why it is so important for suffering people to be able to look at Christians and see a desirable state in which peace and fulfillment can be readily seen. They need to be able to recognize that the Christian's hole has been filled with something that fits so perfectly, the emptiness can no longer be seen. Surprisingly, one person that saw this search and need for being filled by God was Carl Jung, one of the forefathers of modern psychiatry. The following quote from a letter written from Carl Jung to Bill Wilson illustrates his belief.

> "His craving for alcohol was the equivalent on a low level of the spiritual thirst of our being for wholeness, expressed in medieval language: the union with God.
>
> I am strongly convinced that the evil principle prevailing in this world leads the unrecognized spiritual need into perdition, if it is not counteracted by a real religious insight or by the protective wall of human community. An ordinary man, not protected by an action from above and isolated in society, cannot resist the power of evil, which is very aptly called the devil.
>
> Alcohol in Latin is spiritus, and you use the same word for the highest religious experience as well as for the most depraving poison.
>
> 'As the heart panteth after the water brooks, so panteth my soul after thee, O God.' Psalm 42:1" (Pass It On, page 384)

Pages 382–386 of "Pass It On" contain the full exchange of letters between Bill Wilson and Carl Jung, and they make for very interesting reading. The big problem with getting someone to reach out and ask for what Jesus has to offer in the first place, is denial.

Denial is a powerful force. It is simply amazing how messed up someone's life can be, yet they will look you straight in the eye and say they don't have a problem. They really believe no one can see their problem. If you ignore a problem, maybe it will go away. Humankind has been trying to hide from their troubles ever since the third chapter of Genesis.

> *"When they heard the sound of God strolling in the garden in the evening breeze, the man and his wife hid in the trees of the garden, hid from God."*
> *(Genesis 3:8 MES)*

Hiding from devastating problems today has about the same effect as it did then. The consequences catch up with the person in trouble in spite of their denial. Of course, it is still nice to have someone else to blame, just as it was then.

> *"The man said, 'The woman you put here with me–she gave me some fruit from the tree, and I ate it.'"*
> *(Genesis 3:12 NIV)*

What this demonstrates is the next line of defense after it becomes obvious there is a problem: blame someone else. Actually, it appears that Adam is not only blaming Eve, he is blaming God for making Eve. This gives the person a reason for not doing anything about the problem. It is no longer about them; it is about someone else and is therefore out of their hands. Here are some common examples of blaming others. "If only my wife hadn't left me, I could stop drinking." "I could quit drinking if only my wife would leave me." "If you had a wife like mine, you would drink too." "God has it in for me." Blaming others also excuses behavior by saying anyone would behave like this in my situation. The basic purpose for denying a problem exists or blaming others for the problem, is to avoid confronting the problem.

People know they have problems and in the back of their mind, yes, they do want help, but they don't like the fact that they seem to be different from other people. After all, other people don't have a problem with this, so why should they? How far people will go without acknowledging a major problem is amazing, yet it's difficult to change until denial is out of the way and the problem is admitted to and responsibility for the problem is owned. Nothing illustrates this better than the following two paragraphs from the "Big Book" of Alcoholics Anonymous.

> "Most of us have been unwilling to admit we were real alcoholics. No person likes to think he is bodily and mentally different from his fellows. Therefore, it is not surprising that our drinking careers have been characterized by countless vain attempts to prove we could drink like other people. The idea that somehow, someday he will control and enjoy his drinking is the great obsession of every abnor-

mal drinker. The persistence of this illusion is astonishing. Many pursue it into the gates of insanity or death.

We learned that we had to fully concede to our innermost selves that we were alcoholics. This is the first step in recovery. The delusion that we are like other people, or presently may be, has to be smashed." (Alcoholics Anonymous. page 30)

Even though alcoholics are different than other people in the ability to take or leave a drink, they are more similar than they are different. It is human nature to deny we have problems. All of us have some sort of problems and human nature seems to whisper in our ear, if you don't acknowledge it, it isn't real. What usually needs to happen before we humans reach out for help is, we need to hit bottom. Hitting bottom means we can't bare our troubles any longer, the burden is far too heavy and we are about to be crushed. Oftentimes this person has lost nearly everything except their life and don't really care if they loose it. This is the place Bill Wilson had arrived at when he cried out for God and had the spiritual experience described in a previous chapter.

This brings up the question, does everyone need to get to such a desperate place before asking for help. The answer thankfully is no. Human beings have many negative tendencies, but along with them they have the ability to learn. We have already determined that people have a desire to get better even if this desire is buried under a load of sin. If they can be shown that others have been on the same path, have not been able to recover on their own and have lost everything before reaching out to God for help, they may see the light and turn around before things reach an absolute bottom. This is referred to as raising someone's bottom. This is the basic principle behind sentencing people to jail for driving under the influence charges and then offering them drug and alcohol treatment instead. Hopefully, they will learn where the path they are on will inevitably lead and make a decision to turn around before they reach absolute bottom. This principle is at work in twelve step meetings as well. By going to meetings and hearing the stories of others, a person can see where they are headed and turn around sooner.

This is another reason it is helpful for people in the Christian community to expand their knowledge of the common problems that destroy people's lives. By educating yourself, you can help educate others and perhaps be a part of raising their bottom. A word of warning though: don't judge and don't take an inventory of what's wrong in their life's for them, just help them to take their own inventory by listening, talking and if the opportunity presents its self, sharing some of a testimony you have heard from others that may parallel theirs.

When you think about it, much of the Bible is devoted to this purpose. Consider Proverbs and Ecclesiastes. King Solomon has made many mistakes and traveled down many paths that were meaningless. He has also observed anti-productive behavior in many of his subjects. His goal in presenting this information to us is to help us see the end of the path we are on, so we don't have to travel clear to the end, only to be met with disappointment. The Bible helps us to see the need to turn from sin, before it completely destroys us.

Hurting people do want to feel better, they just don't know how. Oftentimes they have struggled for years with a problem and tried everything they could think of to make things better. As long as they continue to look in themselves for the answer, they will only find more misery. With a gentle understanding approach, informed Christians can gently point them to a healing power outside of them, the awesome healing power of Jesus Christ.

Most Alcoholics have vowed to never drink again dozens, if not hundreds, of times and have meant it every time. They do want help; they just don't know where to look. Many other problems follow the same pattern. Hurting people do want help; they just don't know what help looks like.

## 5. My Experience Strength and Hope

By this time you are likely wondering who I am and where this information comes from. I truly believe the information in this book comes from God. He has used the last forty-five years to convey it to me. Some of the lessons have been difficult ones and at times I have felt forsaken, but with hindsight, I can honestly say that God has never forsaken me. The times in my life where God was difficult to see were the result of my looking in a different direction. God has always been there and I know that He always will be.

A while back, the Lord led me to share my testimony in my church. The best way for me to introduce myself to you would be to share that testimony with you. It will repeat some things discussed elsewhere in this book and it may not fit the flow of the book perfectly, but I wanted to share it with you in its entirety, just the way I shared it that day in church. I was very humbled by and grateful for the opportunity to share it with my church family and I feel the same about sharing it with you. My prayer is that God will use what I have been through to improve the life of others.

I was born into a rural Minnesota farm family. We were very regular attendees of a small country Lutheran church, a short way from our home. As a child, life consisted of three things: church, school and a never-ending supply of farm work.

Knowledge of the Bible and Christ's message of forgiveness were attained through Sunday school, church and Billy Graham crusades on the one available TV channel. At the age of accountability, when first able to comprehend this message, I asked for forgiveness through Jesus and have been a Christian all my life. An active prayer life filled with compassion and concern for others soon followed and continued to develop into my early teen years. Along with the message of a loving God however, came a message of a vengeful, judgmental God that needed in some way to be feared and could quite possibly strike a person with lightning if they were bad.

I was always very sensitive and cried easily, something I soon learned would be met with ridicule from my father and from society as a whole. Intense feelings at times seemed to overwhelm me, and attempting to suppress them appeared to be the best defense against being teased, but I wasn't very good at it. Apparently, being from a family with a publicly judgmental, perfectionist father, who never missed church, never drank or smoked and at least professed to not use profanity, were also reasons for being teased.

At times, small groups of young adults would come around to our church, sharing their testimony and spending time with the young people of the church. They often had dramatic testimonies of a troubled youth ending at the exact date, time and place they were saved, followed by a dramatic turn around in which problems seemed to disappear from their life in an instant. I remember complaining to God about how boring my witness was. How could my uneventful testimony ever compare to the excitement of theirs.

I had tried alcohol once but wasn't very impressed with how sick it made me, and had smoked a few cigarettes. Other than that it had been the straight and narrow. At the age of fifteen I began to hear talk of something called marijuana. Despite strong warnings from various adults, it seemed harmless enough to give it a try.

The first time I smoked pot, I made an amazing discovery. It allowed me to suppress my feelings. It also produced a euphoric feeling that offered an escape from reality for a short time and it didn't make me sick like alcohol had. It created a state where thought without emotion was possible. I was no longer on the verge of tears and as a bonus, the same people that used to tease me seemed to gain respect for me.

From that time on, every opportunity to smoke pot was taken. Within a year, daily use had become the norm, often starting before school in the morning. This soon gave way to the use of stronger drugs like speed, LSD and angel dust. As a senior I enlisted in the Army and decided it was time to learn to drink alcohol and added that to the mix. However, marijuana always remained my drug of choice.

During this time, my prayer life and church

attendance had ceased to exist. I was afraid that if I talked to God, it would call His attention to me and He would be reminded about throwing the lightning bolts. Through all my years of drug use, I never denounced God, always considered myself a Christian and believe had my life ended, Jesus would have taken me to heaven, but my fig leaf was quite large.

By the time I was 20 years old it was glaringly obvious I was in the midst of a severe drug problem. I had quit every extra curricular activity in my senior year of high school, been in and out of the Army, spent time in jail, was on probation and had tried and failed an attempt at college. I really wanted things to be different. The resolve to change my life was very real. This produced my first exposure to the twelve steps of Alcoholics Anonymous.

They appeared to be useful; the lives of the people talking about them seemed to be going well. It was exciting and my hopes were high. My father said I needed to quit drugs, drinking and smoking, straighten out my life, and then go to church. I began again to try to develop the type of relationship with God the successful people in my family seemed to have, yet I felt less than them, judged, and defiantly not understood or accepted.

For a while my life appeared to be going better, but as time went by, I thought more and more about smoking a joint; it was as if pot would talk to me, telling me I could use it in moderation and everything would be fine. It said I had surely learned my lesson and could now be a responsible user. It even used my name. Once I gave in, it was too late; back came the fear of God and up went the fig leaf. Use in moderation was short lived and daily use was back.

The next 16 years were littered with countless attempts to quit and every time I really meant it. Many times I would drag myself back to a twelve step group. I tried inpatient drug and alcohol treatment, going to church, counseling, going back to school, changing where I lived, etc. The results, however, were always the same: a return to daily drug use. I was utterly defeated and convinced that this drug use was something I would have with me the rest of my life. I had tried everything I could think of, the drugs were simply more powerful than me.

During this time I had gotten married and had two children. I loved my family dearly but had a hard time expressing it. The drugs caused me to be emotionally unavailable and of course took money that could have gone elsewhere. I liked being married, loved my wife and dreamed of some day being old and gray together, sitting in our rockers, with grandkids on our laps. When it became obvious that our nine year relationship was going to end in divorce, the pain was unbearable. It felt as if I was being crushed and turned to my old friend marijuana for help, but discovered that the feelings were so intense no amount of drugs and alcohol could suppress them.

One day while laying in the back yard under the weight of this great burden, I screamed out to

God that I couldn't take the pain any more and that He simply had to do something. The fig leaf dropped off. The lightning bolt would have been a welcome change to how I was feeling. That was the first time in my life I ever talked with God while stoned. No lightning bolt came, in fact nothing spectacular happened at all, yet from somewhere the strength to get up and continue through the things that needed to be done, came.

In the days and weeks to come I continued to smoke pot and became even further convinced that this unwanted companion would be with me the rest of my life. The one thing different was I continued to talk with God in spite of my altered state and to my delight I felt loved and accepted, not judged and condemned.

One evening, at the time of God's choosing, Jesus came to me and said, "Alvin, it's time to turn a new page in your life, you won't need the pot anymore." My first reaction was disbelief. In fact, I tried to light a joint, but couldn't. The next day I went through the house rounding up everything associated with smoking pot and discarded it. From that moment on, I have never been seriously tempted to smoke it again. Eventually, God convinced me of the need to give up drinking as well. Miraculously, thanks to the absolute power and grace of God, I have been drug and alcohol free for nearly ten years.

Regular attendance at some sort of twelve step meeting seemed important and very helpful. I finally understood the first step: the power to defeat my addiction simply was not in me, I was and still am powerless. The second step showed me that God could and would help if only I would ask. I wouldn't be cured of my addiction, only granted a daily reprieve contingent on the maintenance of my spiritual condition. This pointed to the need of seeking God's grace on a daily basis.

I remained confused about God, yet felt bad for those poor souls for whom the phrase "God, as we understood Him" had been created. Certainly, with all the knowledge of the Bible and religious background in my childhood, I understood God the "right way." Then one day as I listened at a meeting it hit me like a ton of bricks, that "right way" of understanding God, the understanding that involved fear, shame, guilt and hiding. The one that said God would show me favor if only I did things more like my brother, you know, the "right way" hadn't been working so well. I realized that I had been trying to use someone else's understanding of God and what really needed to be done, if I wanted to remain sober, was to develop my own understanding of God.

This attitude at times seemed to unnerve certain people in my life and at family functions I went from being a hopeless, useless drug addict to being branded as a heretic. I actually felt more rejected from some of my religious relatives now than when stoned. Some even said that because I didn't see God exactly as they did, I was evil.

This journey of new understanding has unveiled a very loving, caring, forgiving and compassionate

God. A God there is no need do fear or feel shame in front of; that wants a personal relationship with me; that is ready at any moment, if I ask, to put the most powerful force in the universe to work on my problems; that will give me all the second chances I need, and will bless my life beyond belief, if only I will get out of His way. Obviously, developing a relationship with this loving God would be the first step in dealing with my brokenness, not the last as my father had seemed to suggest by saying I needed to quit my bad habits and then go to church.

In my fourth year of sobriety, I was simply amazed at what God had done in my life. I had gone back to school and was nearing my BA degree, was quite involved in twelve step service work, had held various service positions and currently represented my district at area functions. I attended many twelve step meetings, and had a lot of good friends. My conscious contact with God was at an all time high.

As the fifth year of sobriety neared, I was becoming more and more aware that something was wrong with me. I had spells of dizziness, nausea and fatigue. It was becoming harder to be around people. Any sort of conflict was difficult to deal with. As things worsened, I was forced to resign my service position and felt I had let the twelve step community down. It was even getting more and more difficult to go to meetings. In fact, a time was coming where I wanted desperately to go to meetings, but simply could not for almost a year. I had to give up school eight credits short of my BA. It got to the point where

I simply couldn't leave home. If someone drove in the yard, I hid.

As things worsened, I began to seek medical help. After a trail of doctors and specialists, taking a MMPI was recommended. This of course sounded like a waste of time because I could not possibly have a mental illness, but I took it. It diagnosed panic disorder, with agoraphobia and depression. This put me in front of a psychiatrist, a place that society had taught me no self-respecting person with any strength and substance would ever be. Many medication attempts were made with poor results. I had fallen into the deepest, darkest pit imaginable. When bad days turned into bad weeks, then into bad months, I began to wonder what the point of continuing to live was. My disability was considered by the doctors to be total and permanent and the prognosis was poor. I had become extremely angry and bitter toward God. Why was he doing this to me after all I had already suffered?

This led to working with a PhD level psychologist. We did a lot of work. One of first things she did was help me get back on track spiritually by encouraging my return to a twelve step meeting. She convinced me to further discuss my physical symptoms with a general practitioner, and finally to go back to the psychiatrist for another medication trial. This time I could tell things were different, that this medication would really help.

In the last few years, I have worked harder than ever on recovery. Not just recovery from drug and alcohol abuse, but total recovery. This includes physical, mental, emotional and spiritual recovery. The results have been miraculous. Again God has done for me what I could not do for myself. The doctors are amazed. My psychiatrist, the same one that at one time thought my illness hopeless and a waste of his time, said I could be a poster child for recovery.

Gradually, the ability to function in public places returned on a limited basis. I used to take the ability to leave home for granted. Today I know that it is an absolute privilege to have the ability to attend twelve step meetings and church. My conscious contact with God, as I understand him, is at a new and ever increasing level. When I see people suffering from ailments similar to what I have been through, which is surprisingly common, I can't help but share my experience, strength and especially hope with them. I would not trade lives with anyone. I love who I am and what I've been through. Were it not for the pain in my life, I would not have this insight, understanding, compassion and love for those who still suffer. I have been given a tremendous gift and hope that God will use me to touch others the way he has touched me.

Many people have asked if I caused my mental illness with all the drug abuse. Doctors and mental health professionals say it's the other way around, the mental illness caused the drug abuse. The drug abuse had been an attempt to self-medicate the illness. The course my life has taken is not due to stupidity, weakness or bad choices, although I do admit to making many bad choices and sometimes still do. It is due to physiological factors I was born with, such as a genetic predisposition to depression and anxiety, coupled with the environmental factors in my childhood.

Many people seem to believe this is an excuse for poor behavior. It is not, it is an explanation of that behavior, which leads to understanding and understanding leads to less fear, and with less fear it is easier to ask for help. This does not mean a person that has done something wrong should be excused from the consequences of their behavior. In fact, going through the consequences caused by damaging behavior can be very valuable to a person's recovery.

One of the biggest lessons I have learned reminds me that it is by the grace of God that I am not worse off: many people do have graver ailments and less ability than me. If one chooses to look for what's wrong with life, there is plenty to be found, but this will lead to misery. The choice to see what is positive, right and good in life, which leads to happiness, can also be made. Whether I look at life with a positive or negative perspective is, with the help of God, something over which I have some control.

Through my years of involvement in twelve step programs, I have learned to be very grateful for all the gifts God has given me. I have gotten to know God, myself and others in a very loving way. I have been given reasonable happiness. I can recognize my feelings and embrace them as my friends. The sensitivity God instilled in me is a good thing. I know now that real men do cry. Perhaps the greatest gift God has given me through the twelve step process is peace of mind.

A big contribution to this peace of mind comes from learning to forgive, love and pray for those that have hurt me the most. At the time of my father's death a year ago, God had enabled me to work out the relationship with my father so I was able to say goodbye in love, with no ill feelings. I have also been able to get to a point where I harbor no ill feelings toward my ex-wife and actually wish her well. When I notice ill feelings toward anyone, I know its time to work on forgiving them and find the best way of doing this is to pray for God's blessing on their life.

Another important concept spoke of in twelve step programs is the claim of spiritual progress rather than spiritual perfection and that three steps forward and two steps back is still progress. God is delighted when there is progress in my life and does not expect perfection. He just wants me to keep working on it to the best of my ability.

I now see that all people are in the same boat; we all have circumstances in our life that are out of our control. We all have hurts, habits or hang-ups and need the power of God to deal with them. The twelve step process can help anyone, regardless of their circumstances, achieve a more peaceful and meaning-filled life.

When you hear about a "twelve step program," you probably think it's a good thing because it's helped all those alcoholics and addicts, yet since you are not an addict or alcoholic, there would be little to gain from the twelve steps. You may have also heard it's kind of secular, referring to some sort of "Higher Power" or "God, as we understand Him."

The truth is, alcohol is mentioned only one time in the twelve steps as they were originally written by Bill Wilson, cofounder of Alcoholics Anonymous. In fact, the twelve steps are not about quitting drinking at all. They are about learning a new "God centered" way of life. God is referred to eight times in the twelve steps.

The twelve steps come directly from the Bible and each step can be easily backed up with many Bible verses. It is commonly said that the three places in the Bible most closely linked with the twelve step way of life are the Beatitudes (Matthew chapter 5), I Corinthians 13 (the love chapter) and the book of James which advocates taking action.

The first step states, "We admitted we were powerless over alcohol; that our lives had become unmanageable." If the word "alcohol" is replaced with the word "sin," the twelve steps become a blueprint for a more effective Christian life. The phrases "God, as we understand Him" and "Higher Power" are used to gently ease people into the idea of a personal relationship with God. Many of the people coming to twelve step groups, would be scared off by a more Biblical or religious approach; in time, however, a lot of these people end up with a strong Christian faith.

*12 Steps*
TO A MORE EFFECTIVE CHRISTIAN WITNESS

Oftentimes groups like AA can help people the church hasn't been able to reach, by accepting them just as they are and gently supporting their desire to improve by setting a good example and listening to problems with a non-judgmental ear. People do best when encouraged to take their own inventory and are often pushed away by someone else taking it for them.

In a nutshell, the twelve steps teach us to "trust God, clean house, help others." In other words, we trust God to guide us through a process of self examination in which we identify our weaknesses, strengths and un-confessed sin. Then we deal with them in a way that lightens the burdens we carry and deepens our relationship with God, ourselves and other people. As a result, we become more useful to God in carrying His message to those who still suffer. As Jesus instructed, we take the log out of our own eye before helping with the speck in our neighbor's eye.

As a result of incorporating the twelve steps into your life, God will bless you in ways you have never imagined. You will achieve a deeper sense of serenity and peace of mind than you ever thought possible. You will have a better understanding of who you are as well as why you are. You will see that God is longing to do things for you that you cannot do for yourself; wonderful things you have never dreamed of will happen in your life. You will become a part of the miracles God is working in the lives of others; nothing in this life is a greater privilege than that.

## 6. Steps and Prayers

Before continuing the journey deeper into the steps, it's important that everyone know what the twelve steps are. Many people know them or at least have an idea of what they are. Regardless of where you are with your knowledge of them, it's good to read them again. At the beginning of an AA meeting, "How it works" from pages 58–60 of the "Big Book" of Alcoholics Anonymous is read. This is the first place the world ever saw the twelve steps. The following excerpt containing the twelve steps and the few paragraphs before and after still appear the same in the fourth addition of the "Big Book" as they did when originally published in 1939. This is exactly, word for word, what is read near the beginning every AA meeting.

## How it Works

Rarely have we seen a person fail who has thoroughly followed our path. Those who do not recover are people who cannot or will not completely give themselves to this simple program, usually men and women who are constitutionally incapable of being honest with themselves. There are such unfortunates. They are not at fault; they seem to have been born that way. They are naturally incapable of grasping and developing a manner of living which demands rigorous honesty. Their chances are less than average. There are those, too, who suffer from grave emotional and mental disorders, but many of them do recover if they have the capacity to be honest.

Our stories disclose in a general way what we used to be like, what happened, and what we are like now. If you have decided you want what we have and are willing to go to any length to get it–then you are ready to take certain steps.

At some of these we balked. We thought we could find an easier, softer way. But we could not. With all the earnestness at our command, we beg of you to be fearless and thorough from the very start. Some of us have tried to hold on to our own ideas and the result was nil until we let go absolutely.

Remember that we deal with alcohol–cunning, baffling, powerful! Without help it is too much for us. But there is one who has all power–that one is God. May you find Him now!

Half measures availed us nothing. We stood at the turning point. We asked His protection and care with complete abandon.

Here are the steps we took which are suggested as a program of recovery:

1. We admitted we were powerless over alcohol–that our lives had become unmanageable.

2. Came to believe that a Power greater than ourselves could restore us to sanity.

3. Made a decision to turn our will and our lives over to the care of God *as we understood Him.*

4. Made a shearing and fearless moral inventory of ourselves.

5. Admitted to God, to ourselves, and to another human being the exact nature of our wrongs.

6. Were entirely ready to have God remove all these defects of character.

7. Humbly asked Him to remove our shortcomings.

8. Made a list of all persons we had harmed, and became willing to make amends to them all.

9. Made direct amends to such people wherever possible, except when to do so would injure them or others.

10. Continued to take personal inventory and when we were wrong promptly admitted it.

11. Sought through prayer and meditation to improve our conscious contact with God *as we understood Him,* praying only for knowledge of His will for us and the power to carry that

out.

12. Having had a spiritual awakening as the result of these steps, we tried to carry this message to alcoholics, and to practice these principles in all our affairs.

Many of us exclaimed, "What an order! I can't go through with it." Do not be discouraged. No one among us has been able to maintain anything like perfect adherence to these principles. We are not saints. The point is, that we are willing to grow along spiritual lines. The principles we have set down are guides to progress. We claim spiritual progress rather than spiritual perfection.

Our description of the alcoholic, the chapter to the agnostic, and our personal adventures before and after make clear three pertinent ideas:

(a) That we were alcoholics and could not manage our own lives.

(b) That probably no human power could have relieved our alcoholism.

(c) That God could and would if He were sought. (Alcoholics Anonymous pages 58–60)

---

What a powerful grouping of words! Certainly these words give us all something to work on for the rest of the time God sees fit to leave us here. It is easy to think these words were written for alcoholics, and wonder what benefit they could hold for me. Let's have some fun and at the same time become more familiar with the twelve steps while answering what benefit they could hold for you. Here they are again, only this time, forget you ever heard of Alcoholics Anonymous or alcoholism. Pretend you ran across this set of words in a Bible study at church. To make this exercise easier, I have deleted six words and added six words. See if you can tell where they are:

---

## How it works

Rarely have we seen a person fail who has thoroughly followed our path. Those who do not recover are people who cannot or will not completely give themselves to this simple program, usually men and women who are constitutionally incapable of being honest with themselves. There are such unfortunates. They are not at fault; they seem to have been born that way. They are naturally incapable of grasping and developing a manner of living which demands rigorous honesty. Their chances are less than average. There are those, too, who suffer from grave emotional and mental disorders, but many of them do recover if they have the capacity to be honest.

Our stories disclose in a general way what we used to be like, what happened, and what we are like now. If you have decided you want what we have and are willing to go to any length to get it–then you are ready to take certain steps.

*12 Steps*
TO A MORE EFFECTIVE CHRISTIAN WITNESS

At some of these we balked. We thought we could find an easier, softer way. But we could not. With all the earnestness at our command, we beg of you to be fearless and thorough from the very start. Some of us have tried to hold on to our own ideas and the result was nil until we let go absolutely.

Remember that we deal with sin–cunning, baffling, powerful! Without help it is too much for us. But there is one who has all power–that one is God. May you find Him now!

Half measures availed us nothing. We stood at the turning point. We asked His protection and care with complete abandon.

Here are the steps we took which are suggested as a program of recovery:

1. We admitted we were powerless over sin–that our lives had become unmanageable.

2. Came to believe that a Power greater than ourselves could restore us to sanity.

3. Made a decision to turn our will and our lives over to the care of God *as we understood Him.*

4. Made a shearing and fearless moral inventory of ourselves.

5. Admitted to God, to ourselves, and to another human being the exact nature of our wrongs.

6. Were entirely ready to have God remove all these defects of character.

7. Humbly asked Him to remove our shortcomings.

8. Made a list of all persons we had harmed, and became willing to make amends to them all.

9. Made direct amends to such people wherever possible, except when to do so would injure them or others.

10. Continued to take personal inventory and when we were wrong promptly admitted it.

11. Sought through prayer and meditation to improve our conscious contact with God *as we understood Him,* praying only for knowledge of His will for us and the power to carry that out.

12. Having had a spiritual awakening as the result of these steps, we tried to carry this message to people, and to practice these principles in all our affairs.

Many of us exclaimed, "What an order! I can't go through with it." Do not be discouraged. No one among us has been able to maintain anything like perfect adherence to these principles. We are not saints. The point is, that we are willing to grow along spiritual lines. The principles we have set down are guides to progress. We claim spiritual progress rather than spiritual perfection.

Our description of the sinner, the chapter to the agnostic, and our personal adventures before and after make clear three pertinent ideas:

(a) That we were sinners and could not manage our own lives.

(b) That no human power could have relieved our sin nature.

(c) That God could and would if He were sought.

---

Did you catch the changes? They are subtle. Do you see anything that doesn't belong in any Christian church? Maybe you are thinking the phrase "as we understood Him" doesn't belong. It does at times seem to make some Christians uncomfortable. Think about this; do you understand God in the exact same way today as you did months or years ago? Do you think your understanding of God will be different a year from now? Do you think your understanding of God may be slightly different from that of your pastor? Is your understanding of God a little different from that of your other family members? Yet many of these understandings seem to be valid. The important thing is that we have some kind of understanding of God. This current understanding is a point to grow from and none of us will ever have a perfect understanding of God, because our finite mind will never be able to fully comprehend an infinite God.

Sometimes we fail to see the big picture because we are hung up on some small detail, a detail that doesn't really make a lot of difference. The big picture is every human being that ever lived, or will live, would benefit greatly from the attempted practice of the twelve steps. This will never happen of course, but even one more person living the kind of life God has instructed us to live is progress, progress that makes this world just a little nicer place to be.

After some thought and study, it is easy to see why the twelve steps have been adopted by so many different groups: they work for any problem a person is having. There is one more version of the twelve steps for you to consider. The reason for using this version is because they have done a wonderful job of comparing each step to scripture. The following is how the twelve steps appear in each of the four Celebrate Recovery participant's guides. Please read through them one more time.

## TWELVE STEPS
## *with Biblical Comparisons*

1.  We admitted we were powerless over our addictions and compulsive behaviors, that our lives had become unmanageable.
    *I know that nothing good lives in me, that is,*

*in my sinful nature. For I have the desire to do what is good, but I cannot carry it out.*
*Romans 7:18*

2. We came to believe that a power greater than ourselves could restore us to sanity.
   *For it is God who works in you to will and to act according to His good purpose.*
   *Philippians 2:13*

3. We made a decision to turn our wills and our lives over to the care of God.
   *Therefore, I urge you, brothers, in view of God's mercy, to offer your bodies as living sacrifices, holy and pleasing to God—this is your spiritual act of worship.*
   *Romans 12:1*

4. We made a searching and fearless moral inventory of ourselves.
   *Let us examine our ways and test them, and let us return to the Lord.*
   *Lamentations 3:40*

5. We admitted to God, to ourselves, and to another human being the exact nature of our wrongs.
   *Therefore confess your sins to each other and pray for each other so that you may be healed.*
   *James 5:16*

6. We were entirely ready to have God remove all these defects of character.
*Humble yourselves before the Lord, and He will lift you up.*
*James 4:10*

7. We humbly ask Him to remove all our shortcomings.
*If we confess our sins, He is faithful and just and will forgive us our sins and purify us from all unrighteousness.*
*1 John 1:9*

8. We made a list of all persons we had harmed and became willing to make amends to them all.
*Do to others as you would have them do to you.*
*Luke 6:31*

9. We made direct amends to such people whenever possible, except when to do so would injure them or others.
*Therefore, if you are offering your gift at the altar and there remember that your brother has something against you, leave your gift there in front of the altar. First go and be reconciled to your brother; then come and offer your gift.*
*Matthew 5:23–24*

10. We continued to take personal inventory and when we were wrong, promptly admitted it.

*So if you think you are standing firm, be careful that you don't fall.*
1 Corinthians 10:12

**11.** We sought through prayer and meditation to improve our conscious contact with God, praying only for knowledge of His will for us and the power to carry that out.
*Let the word of Christ dwell in you richly.*
*Colossians 3:16*

**12.** Having had a spiritual experience as a result of these steps, we tried to carry this message to others and to practice these principles in all our affairs.
*Brothers, if someone is caught in a sin, you who are spiritual should restore him gently. But watch yourself, or you also may be tempted.*
*Galatians 6:1*

(Celebrate Recovery, Participants guide 1 pages 11–12)

---

By now you can see just how Biblically based the twelve steps really are. Along with the twelve steps there are some prayers that are commonly associated with twelve step groups. Every AA meeting that I know of is opened by everyone joining together in the first four lines of the serenity prayer, and closed with everyone holding hands while reciting the Lord's Prayer. This holding of hands while saying the Lord's Prayer really produces a feeling of spiritual connectedness, especially when it is done at an event with several hundred in attendance. It is really cool.

The interesting thing about the serenity prayer is how many people think that the first four lines are all there is to it, and how surprised they are to find out there's more. After hearing the rest of the prayer for the first time, they tend to be quite moved and usually ask for copies. Here is the entire serenity prayer:

## PRAYER FOR SERENITY

God grant me the serenity
to accept the things I cannot change,
the courage to change the things I can,
and the wisdom to know the difference.
Living one day at a time,
enjoying one moment at a time;
accepting hardship as a pathway to peace;
taking, as Jesus did,
this sinful world as it is,
not as I would have it;
trusting that You will make all things right
if I surrender to Your will;
so that I may be reasonably happy in this life
and supremely happy with You forever in the next.
Amen.

Reinhold Niebuhr

There is so much content in this prayer that I hope you will re-read it a couple of times, stopping to ponder each line as you go through it. The thing that seems to jump out to most people is the phrase "reasonably happy," indicating that into every life here on earth, some darkness may fall, but with the love of God we can find reasonable happiness in the midst of such darkness.

There are also prayers associated with three of the steps. The following is referred to as the third step prayer and is found in the "Big Book" of Alcoholics Anonymous.

"God I offer myself to thee–to build with me and to do with me as thou wilt. Relieve me of the bondage of self, that I may better do thy will. Take away my difficulties, that victory over them may bear witness to those I would help of Thy Power, Thy Love, and Thy Way of life. May I do Thy will always!" (Alcoholics Anonymous page 63)

If you haven't noticed by now, there is a very strong emphasis in the twelve steps and in twelve step literature on surrendering to God's will. This is because the authors of this material have found out through years of alcohol abuse that their own will is what got them into the mess they were in. Therefore, it only seems logical to assume more of the same (their will) would bring more of the same (A big mess!).

The seventh step prayer continues with this theme. It is also found in the "Big Book" of Alcoholics Anonymous and goes like this:

"My Creator, I am now willing that you should have all of me, good and bad. I pray that you now remove from me every single defect of character which stands in the way of my usefulness to you and my fellows. Grant me strength, as I go from here, to do your bidding. Amen." (Alcoholics Anonymous page 76)

Along with this theme of seeking God's will is a theme of thinking of others instead of thinking of yourself. When concentrating on God's will, helping others always seems to come up. This takes us back to why God leaves us here once we are saved–to help spread the love of Christ to others. No prayer has ever voiced this better then the prayer of St Francis, which is the prayer chosen for study when attempting to understand the eleventh step. The following version can be found in "Twelve Steps and Twelve Traditions":

"Lord, make me a channel of thy peace– that where there is hatred, I may bring love– that where there is wrong, I may bring the spirit of forgiveness that where there is discord, I may bring harmony–that where there is error, I may bring truth–that where there is doubt, I may bring faith–that where there is despair, I may bring hope–that where there are shadows, I may bring light–that where there is sadness, I may bring joy. Lord, grant that I may seek rather to comfort than to be comforted–to understand, than to be understood–to love, than to be loved. For it is by self-forgetting that one finds. It is by forgiving that one is forgiven. It is by dying that one awakens to eternal life. Amen." (Twelve Steps and Twelve Traditions page 99)

This is truly why we as Christians are here, to reach out to hurting people in any way that helps them catch a glimpse of God's unending love. To be a channel of God's peace, the peace that passes all understanding.

When all these steps and prayers are brought together in one place it can be somewhat overwhelming. The reasoning behind presenting them together is so you can more easily find them again. There is enough in this chapter to work on for a lifetime, and if you take the time to come back and meditate on them from time to time, it will have a wonderful effect on you, drawing you nearer to God than you ever thought possible, and there is no better place to be!

## 7. The Twelve Step Community

Many people do not realize the scope of the twelve step community. Most places in the United States a person can easily find an AA meeting any evening of the week, well within an hours drive. In most urban areas, within a half hour drive. There are also noon meetings and morning meetings. AA is truly accessible for everyone in this country. The "Big Book" of AA has been translated into many other languages and AA meetings can now be found around the world.

AA members often share experiences they had while traveling in other countries. They commonly share that even though they could not understand the language, they still felt very welcome and at home, that it felt the same. In spite of the lack of verbal communication, on some level they connected with the AA members from their host country. They were able to identify with one another.

It is always a privilege to have guests from other countries attending meetings here as well. Many AA members seek out meetings when they travel and out of town or out of country visitors are common. The point is, the AA community so often spoke of in this book, is truly world wide and encompasses a great number of people, and all of these groups of people are there to apply the same twelve steps to their lives. AA embodies the same spirit throughout the world. When the fourth edition of the "Big Book" of Alcoholics anonymous was released in 2001, the world wide membership of AA was estimated at over two million, consisting of approximately 100,800 groups in about 150 different countries. Approximately twenty-one million copies of the first three editions of the "Big Book" had been distributed.

Now add to that all the other groups that have sprung up using the same twelve steps. There is Narcotics Anonymous, which is a group very parallel to AA in that it helps people with chemical dependency problems including, but not limited to alcohol. They use the basic philosophy that a drug is a drug, including alcohol. If a person has been addicted to one, they need to leave all of them alone and of course work the twelve steps to the best of their ability.

Then there are Gamblers Anonymous, Sex Addicts Anonymous, Over Eaters Anonymous, Alcoholics Victorious, Celebrate Recovery, the list goes on and on. They also have spin-off groups like Alanon, Alateen and Adult Children of Alcoholics, which are designed for people whose lives have been affected by an alcoholic, or the like, in their family. This is what is often referred to as codependency. This is no where near a complete list of all the groups using the twelve steps to help people change their lives for the better, and every one of these groups is pointing its participants toward some kind of personal relationship with a power greater than themselves, a relationship with God.

Very few of these groups define God for the participants, although some, like Alcoholics Victorious and Celebrate Recovery are Christian based and define their higher power as Jesus Christ, but they are the exception, not the rule. This large number of groups presenting a generic God is the reason why an attitude of friendship, respect and understanding from the Christian church is so important. Many of these people are seeking a better understanding of God. Helping these people understand God by picking up where their meetings leave off certainly seems to be the job of the Christian church.

This brings us bluntly to the following questions. Is the twelve step community's use of a generic or undefined God a good thing? Is this just confusing the issue of God? Wouldn't these people be better off left alone until they could come to church and hear the real message of God? Do these types of groups actually keep people away from the church? The simple answers are; yes, no, no, no; answers that deserve to be expanded on.

By using a generic God, twelve step groups avoid the controversy of religion. Even though many of us love our religion and draw many positive things from it, it is important to realize that God and religion is not the same thing. Religion is man made, in that it's mans expression of his interpretation of and beliefs about God. Religion easily gets distracted and off the point. Hundreds of years ago religion, not God, was responsible for the crusades, a horribly dark interpretation of the great commission: if you can't convert them, kill them. A more modern example of religion run amuck is modern terrorists. They are made up largely of Muslim extremists who have hijacked a religion and removed it so far from the love and tolerance of God that no attributes of God remain.

The Christian religions have plenty of ungodly behavior as well. People that look down their noses at anyone not strong enough to help themselves out of trouble. Christians that are so self-righteous and judgmental, they cannot be seen associating with lowly sinners. Christians that seek to control others through the use of shame, guilt and fear. This is just a partial list of the things that lead some people to say, "It's really too bad that Jesus Christ has to be associated with Christianity." Religion always seems to have its share of hypocrisy. We know this hypocrisy is because the Christian church is filled with sinners just like the rest of the human race, but the fact is, many people have been so turned off and pushed away from the Christian church by this hypocrisy, they could never come to a group or meeting they thought to be religious. If twelve step groups all took a religious approach, many of the people that need the compassion and healing power of Jesus Christ the most, would be left out. For many of these people, just the generic God discussed in meetings is enough to make them uncomfortable.

Many people that simply cannot go near a Christian church are introduced to God in the twelve step community and their spiritual growth takes root there. In time, many of these people will find their way to the Christian church if they are made to feel welcome and not looked down upon. In short, the generic approach to God is all inclusive; it enables twelve step groups to reach many people that will not come to church.

As can be seen after becoming familiar with the twelve steps, they are very direct and to the point about what God can and will do for people in need. These groups are not confusing about the power and scope of God at all. They do a very good job of pointing out that God is the only source of strength strong enough to help with overwhelming problems, but again it is God in the generic sense.

As far as leaving them alone until ready to come to church goes, it's not a good idea. Many people would simply never come to church; they just don't consider it a viable solution. You can wait forever and unless someone outside the church points them in the direction of God, creating a curiosity about the Christian church, they would never darken the doors of a Christian church.

The twelve step groups do not keep anyone that is ready to go to church away. Sometimes, people that have had connection to the church in the past and the experience was somewhat pleasurable, will return to church fairly soon. Others that have been more hurt by their association with the Christian church, an all too common situation, may take a good deal longer, but it is not the twelve step group keeping them away, it is actually their past association with the church keeping them away. Thankfully though, as these people get into the making of amends and offering forgiveness stage of the twelve steps, the old wounds begin to heal and they are able to return to the Christian church with a new outlook and an open mind.

Once again they are at a point where the church can help them grow spiritually. These people can tend to be a little oversensitive at first, which is another reason it is so important for long time members of the church to be open, caring, understanding and accepting of people with chips on their shoulder about the Christian church. If they see they were wrong and not all Christians are as judgmental and hypocritical as the people that soured them on the church, you could very well have a new member with a heart for service in your church. If they do, however, run into the negative qualities that turned them away in the first place, it can be a very long time before they try again.

People that have never had any experience with the Christian church have also been pointed toward God. Some never quite make it to the Christian church, but many do develop a curiosity about Christianity after being pointed in the direction of God in their twelve step experience. This is yet another reason to be friendly with the twelve step community, so you can have the opportunity to invite people like this to your church.

The reason many people coming from twelve step groups into the Christian church have such a heart for service is because service to others is emphasized. There is always someone opening up and making coffee for meetings. Normally the chair person for the meetings rotates so everyone gets in on it. Many people get involved in representing their group on a district, area, regional and national level. They often have get-togethers away from the meetings with potluck meals and some kind of program. There is no shortage of people willing to get involved and make these things happen. The biggest dedication of all is that of sponsorship. People often take time to meet with new people outside of meetings, sometimes several times a week and help them better understand the steps or to just listen and talk. They give out their phone numbers and tell new people to call anytime, even in the middle of the night. It is not uncommon for an AA member to crawl out of their warm bed in the middle of the night to go and help someone that they barely know.

Jesus says:

> *"If anyone would come after me, he must deny himself and take up his cross daily and follow me. For whoever wants to save his life will lose it, but whoever loses his life for me will save it. What good is it for a man to gain the whole world, and yet lose or forfeit his very self?"*
> *(Luke 9:23–25 NIV)*

The notes for Luke 9:23 in the NIV study Bible

say, "To follow Jesus requires self-denial, complete dedication and willing obedience." This is not an easy command to follow, yet there are many people in twelve step groups that model this concept well. Giving of one's self to people in need is the ultimate goal of twelve step involvement. Twelve step people are fond of saying, "To keep what you have, you must give it away."

## 8. TWELVE STEP HISTORY

It is impossible to talk about the history and origins of the twelve steps without once again referring to AA. As mentioned earlier, the first time the twelve steps appeared anywhere was in the "Big Book" of Alcoholics Anonymous, first published in 1939. We have also referred to Bill Wilson as a cofounder of AA and the author of the twelve steps, but let's back up a little ways. We already know that Bill Wilson was an out of control drunk that desperately wanted to quit drinking, but could not. He was a very intelligent man who had given little thought to God.

In November of 1934, Bill received a phone call from an old drinking buddy, Ebby T. At that time, Bill and Ebby had not seen each other for five years. Their last meeting had produced a memorable drinking spree that lasted for days and ended in disaster. Ebby wondered if he might come see Bill and two days later he did. Bill noticed something different about Ebby. Bill also noticed he was drinking alone. Bill found this strange, but secretly was happy to have all the booze for himself. When Bill asked what had happened to Ebby, Ebby replied, "I've got religion." This was the last thing that interested Bill, yet the last he had heard of Ebby, he was about to be committed to an asylum for chronic alcoholism.

Ebby went on to share that he had had some visitors from the Oxford Group. The Oxford Group was an evangelistic Christian movement that modeled early Christianity and was not associated with any particular denomination. It was referred to as more of a spiritual movement than a religion. They explained to him that one of their members, Rowland H., had tremendous trouble with alcohol and ended up being treated in Switzerland by the renowned psychiatrist Carl Jung, whose theories can be found in any psychology text book. When treatment with him was failing, Carl Jung told Rowland that he had progressed to a level at which there was little chance for recovery. He then suggested the only hope left was some sort of spiritual awakening and suggested that he immerse himself in an intense religious atmosphere. Upon return to the United States, Rowland ran into the Oxford Group and threw himself headlong into it. To his amazement, he was able to not drink.

Ebby shared that the Oxford Group stressed four principles: absolute honesty, absolute unselfishness, absolute purity and absolute love. They were particularly keen on absolute honesty with God and with one's self. Most importantly, he shared that there were others too that had been able to leave the booze alone. Bill secretly doubted that some of these people had really been heavy drinkers and remained skeptical of this God stuff.

Bill continued to drink, yet he could not get this conversation with his old friend out of his mind. Bill even went to one of the prayer meetings, and in a drunken stupor went forward to receive God. He became more tormented than ever; he wanted what Ebby seemed to have, but couldn't believe in Ebby's God. As his drinking continued, he ended up back in the hospital, a place he had been many times before, under the care of Dr. Silkworth.

Dr. Silkworth had worked with Bill before and at one time held out some hope that Bill would be one of the lucky ones, that because of his intense desire, he could muster up the strength to quit. Now he had given up hope and began to share his theory about alcoholism being more like an allergy than a moral weakness. Once an alcoholic had one drink, he would have an allergic reaction of sorts and was powerless to quit drinking. He compared it to cancer, a progressive disease with no cure. This is the point that Bill Wilson had his conversion experience shared earlier in this book. Never again would Bill doubt the existence of God.

Bill immersed himself in the Biblical atmosphere of the Oxford Group and began his attempt to save the world and all the drunks in it. He had little success, but he was still sober. While out of town on a business trip to Akron, Ohio, Bill was having a bit of a hard time and decided the best thing to do was to find another drunk to work with. He found Dr. Bob Smith. Finally Bill achieved success in helping another drunk sober up and Dr. Bob became a cofounder and the second member of AA. Dr. Bob had his last drink on June tenth, 1935, a date said to be the day AA started.

Dr. Bob and Bill were regular attendees of the

Oxford Group, but as time went on they wanted to concentrate solely on alcoholics and gradually split away from the Oxford Group. The fellowship of AA began to grow in both Akron and New York, Bill's hometown. Eventually they thought it would be good to write down this phenomenal approach to the treating of alcoholism. Bill wrote most of the original text that would become the "Big Book" (Actually named Alcoholics Anonymous) and then presented his drafts to the fellowship for changes and approval.

They decided it would be a good idea to write down this formula in a series of steps. Bill drew on his Oxford Group experience and when he sat down on his bed to write them, the original draft came to him in just a few short minutes. Many people believe that they came out so easily because they were inspired by God. The twelve steps were born. They became official with the publishing of the "Big Book" in 1939.

In the early going there was a lot of excitement about the twelve steps helping anyone with any problem, but through experience, AA decided it was best to do one thing–help people quit drinking, and to do it well. They would have no opinions on other issues, but they would allow anyone else to adapt the twelve steps to whatever problem they wanted to. It is obvious that applying the twelve steps to other problems has been immensely successful; hence the large number of twelve step groups we see today.

The twelve steps would get their first real big test in World War II. Would these men be able to maintain their new found sobriety under the stress of war? A large percent of them did perform admirably and came home sober, able to continue productive, sober lives as civilians. The twelve steps had been proven. They worked then and they still work today, because they are drawn from, and based on, the infallible word of God, the Bible.

In an effort to promote more understanding of the twelve step community it would be helpful to read the twelve traditions of AA. This set of principles was settled upon to guide AA. They were born out of many mistakes and wrong directions. The twelve steps are referred to as "How it works" and the twelve traditions are refereed to as "Why it works," they are as follows.

---

1. Our common welfare should come first; personal recovery depends on AA unity.

2. For our group purpose there is but one ultimate authority–a loving God as He may express Himself in our group conscience.

3. The only requirement for AA membership is a desire to stop drinking.

4. Each group should be autonomous, except in matters affecting other groups or AA as a whole.

*12 Steps*
To a More Effective Christian Witness

5. Each group has but one primary purpose–to carry its message to the alcoholic who still suffers.

6. An AA group ought never endorse, finance, or lend the AA name to any related facility or outside enterprise, lest problems of money, property, and prestige divert us from our primary purpose.

7. Every AA group ought to be fully self-supporting, declining outside contributions.

8. Alcoholics Anonymous should remain forever nonprofessional, but our service centers may employ special workers.

9. AA, as such, ought never be organized; but we may create service boards or committees directly responsible to those they serve.

10. Alcoholics Anonymous has no opinion on outside issues; hence the AA name ought never be drawn into public controversy.

11. Our public relations policy is based on attraction rather than promotion; we need always maintain personal anonymity at the level of press, radio and films.

12. Anonymity is the spiritual foundation of all

our traditions, ever reminding us to place principles before personalities. ("Twelve Steps and Twelve Traditions" pages 9–13)

---

These traditions have guided AA through many years of continued growth. Many people think a study of the traditions will be boring, but as they get into them, they discover that there is much about recovery to be learned from them, especially the lesson of anonymity. It is easy to see that AA wouldn't want someone speaking for them in the press one day and out on a drinking binge the next. It is also understandable that keeping things anonymous helps those who are so terribly embarrassed by how poorly their life has gone feel safe because they know they won't be publicly identified as an AA member. The most important aspect is that of keeping recovering alcoholics humble. Pride is one of the biggest enemies to recovery there is. The moment someone starts thinking how wonderful they are and what great things they are doing in AA, they are in danger of relapse. One of my pastor's favorite acrostics is the one for EGO–_E_dging _G_od _O_ut. It certainly is applicable here. When God's grace heals someone's hurt and gives them the strength to move forward and grow, and then that person's ego edges God out, the supporting strength of the recovery is gone and it collapses.

This is most certainly the principle to which Jesus was referring to in the Sermon on the Mount, when He said:

*"And when you pray, do not be like the hypocrites, for they love to pray standing in the synagogues and on the street corners to be seen by men. I tell you the truth; they have received their reward in full. But when you pray, go into your room, close the door and pray to your father who is unseen. Then your father who sees what is done in secret, will reward you . . . When you fast, do not look somber as the hypocrites do, for they disfigure their faces to show men they are fasting. I tell you the truth, they have received their reward in full. But when you fast, but oil on your head and wash your face, so it will not be obvious to men that you are fasting, but only to your father, who is unseen: and your father who sees what is done in secret, will reward you."*

*(Matthew 6: 5–6 & 16–18 NIV)*

## 9. We Need to Understand Powerlessness

Understanding powerlessness is the crux of the twelve steps. It is also the main theme of Christianity. Were it not for our powerlessness over sin, we would have no need for Jesus. Many people would like to be able to always do what's right and good for them, but they cannot. We are all powerless over sin. Some of us have more trouble with one thing, but not another, where the other thing that we don't struggle with is the downfall of our neighbor. The Bible points this fact out quite clearly in several places. The apostle Paul, in his letter to the Romans, addresses this issue at length. He starts out by giving us a partial list of things we are powerless over.

> *"They have become filled with every kind of wickedness, evil, greed and depravity. They are filled with envy, murder, strife, deceit and malice. They are gossips, slanderers, God haters, insolent, arrogant and boastful; they invent ways of doing evil; they disobey their parents; they are senseless, faithless, heartless, ruthless. Although they know God's righteous decree that those that do such things deserve death, they not only continue to do these very things but also approve of those who practice them."*
> *(Romans 1:28–32 NIV)*

This is a picture of the human race without God. We are powerless to go in any direction other than sin. This is why we need God, not only to insure our place, through grace, with Him in eternity, but to begin to turn away from the awfulness of sin while we are still here. Paul goes on to assure us that we are all in this same boat. In chapter three, he refers back to the Old Testament by saying:

> *"There is no one righteous, not even one; there is no one who understands, no one who seeks God. All have turned away, they have together become worthless; there is no one who does good, not even one."*
> *(Romans 3:10–12 NIV)*

The fact that we are all included comes up once again, but this time is accompanied by the good news of God's unending grace.

> *"This righteousness from God comes through faith in Jesus Christ. There is no difference, [between Jews and gentiles; NIV foot note] for all have sinned and fall short of the glory of God, and are justified freely by His grace through the redemption that came by Jesus Christ."*
> *(Romans 3:22–24 NIV)*

This reiterates what was covered in the "How it works" portion of the "Big Book" of AA: that no human power can save us from sin, but God can and will if He is sought. In this chapter on powerlessness the following verse fits nicely:

> *"You see, at just the right time, when we were still powerless, Christ died for the ungodly."*
> *(Romans 5:6 NIV)*

As we continue through Romans it begins to appear like once we have accepted grace through faith in Jesus Christ, we will no longer sin.

> *"For we know that our old self was crucified with Him so that the body of sin might be done away with, that we should no longer be slaves to sin–because anyone who has died has been freed from sin."*
> *(Romans 6:6–7 NIV)*

This is not what Paul is saying. Being freed from sin means we will spend eternity as coinheritors of the kingdom of God, with Christ. What it means for our time left here on earth, is that when we accept God's grace through faith in Jesus Christ, we begin a journey of spiritual maturation. It means progress, not perfection. The following verses point out a progression rather than an instant change in our sin behavior.

> *"I put this in human terms because*

*you are weak in your natural selves. Just as you used to offer the parts of your body in slavery to impurity and to ever increasing wickedness, so now offer them in slavery to righteousness leading to holiness."*
*(Romans 6:19 NIV)*

*"But now that you have been set free from sin and have become slaves to God, the benefit you reap leads to holiness, and the result is eternal life."*
*(Romans 6:22 NIV)*

Notice the words "leading to holiness" and "leads to holiness." According to the American heritage dictionary, leading means "encouraging a desired response" and lead means "to tend toward a certain goal or result." In other words, we are all works in progress heading toward a sinless existence, but never quite getting there in this lifetime. The following account of Paul's struggle with sin shows just how difficult it is and how powerless Christians are against their sin nature, even after coming to know the Lord.

*"We know that the law is spiritual; but I am unspiritual, sold as a slave to sin. I do not understand what I do. For what I want to do I do not do, but what I hate I do. And if I do what I do not want to do, I agree that the law is good. As it is, it is no longer I*

*myself who do it, but it is sin living in me. I know that nothing good lives in me, that is, in my sinful nature. For I have the desire to do what is good, but I cannot carry it out. For what I do is not the good I want to do; no, the evil I do not want to do–this I keep on doing. Now if I do what I do not want to do, it is no longer I who do it, but it is sin living in me that does it."*
*(Romans 7:14–20 NIV)*

The interesting thing about how Paul goes back and forth, in and out, and over and over this sin in his mind, is that it is the same kind of circling around and around an issue that goes on in the mind of an addict, when they are trying to stay away from their addiction. They are doomed to fail if this train of thought keeps up to long. Their only defense is to turn there confusion about wanting to do what they don't want to do, over to God. He never solves this riddle for them, He just puts their mind on something else, and usually the something else has to do with helping others. When the addict is faithful in following God's request to help others, he finds he is no longer stuck in the juggernaut of mental rumination.

"I am a grateful recovering alcoholic" is often heard echoing around twelve step meetings. It is hard to understand how anyone could have any gratefulness connected with having had their life destroyed by alcohol. Obviously, going through the awful losses caused by addiction in one's life is a horrible, painful thing. However, it is the attitude of many in recovery, that were it not for how obviously out of control their life had gotten, they would have never realized how much they need God in their life. Not only did they need God in beating their addiction, they need him in all facets of their life. The wonderful peace of mind that comes from working the twelve steps and applying them as best they could to all areas of their life is unsurpassed. If not having the pain in their past would mean not having the peace they have now, they would choose to keep the pain and actually become grateful for the pain that led them to the ultimate strength of God.

Anyone who has spent time around an addict of any sort has undoubtedly heard them swear off their addiction. They vow to never do whatever it is that is consuming their life ever again. When they go and do it again the very next day and then promise once more to never do it again, it becomes difficult to believe that they are ever serious about wanting to quit. Many spouses of people caught in the throws of some kind of addiction have heard this pledge to quit hundreds of times. It is easy to pass them off as liars that only say these things to get something out of the person they are making the promise to. The truth is they mean it every time. Not only have they pledged to other people countless times, they have made vows to themselves as well, yet like Paul, they soon find themselves doing what they don't want to do yet again.

It is astonishing how destroyed peoples lives

get before they become willing to go to any lengths to get better. The any length they must go to of course is to form a relationship with God, but this often doesn't happen until the addict has seen over and over and over again , that the power to quit this damaging behavior does not exist inside of him. This concept is even harder to grasp because our society says to pick yourself up, dust yourself off, and move on. Admitting powerlessness is sometimes a very difficult thing to do, but it is the first step to getting better.

If someone in your church or someone you know has tried to get over some problem, seems to be doing good, and then is back into their old behavior, don't be to surprised, backsliding or slipping are common. Addiction to anything is a powerful foe. It is so lucky for us that Jesus is a God of second and two hundred twenty second chances. We need to be the same and welcome anyone back into our churches, no matter how many times they have come and gone, and we need to do it in a loving, supportive, non-judgmental way.

As hard as it is to picture just how powerless people can become over addictions, we as Christians need to come to grips with the fact that we are really all in the same boat. As was pointed out earlier, we all fall short of the glory of God. The part about "everyone of us" is made very clear; there is no room to wiggle out of needing the forgiving, healing power of Jesus Christ. Left to our own devices, we are all powerless over sin!

Just maybe, these poor people that have suffered such great horrors are the lucky ones. Because of their complete defeat, they have learned to depend completely on God. Wouldn't it be nice if more Christians could learn from the lives of these "poor unfortunates" and realize how powerless they are and how much they desperately need God in every aspect of their life, even if, or maybe especially if, their lives seem to be pretty good by worldly standards. Maybe you have more areas of your life that need to be turned over to the loving care of God.

## 10. We Must See Our Own Need First

Before we can help others, we must look at ourselves first. This is why the twelfth step, the one that suggests carrying the message to others in need, is the last step. Certainly, Jesus backed up this order of things when He said:

> *"Why do you look at the speck of sawdust in your brother's eye and pay no attention to the plank in your own eye? How can you say to your brother, "Let me take the speck out of your eye," when all the time there is a plank in your own eye? You hypocrite, first take the plank out of your own eye, and then you will see clearly to remove the speck from your brothers eye."*
> *(Matthew 7:3–5 NIV)*

People can smell hypocrisy a mile away. Remember the old saying, "What's good for the goose is good for the gander." Why would you bother giving someone else advice that you are not willing to follow yourself. Some people will say to this, "But I don't have the severity of problems that he or she does." This attitude points to the lack of believing we are all in the same boat. Again, we all sin; we are all powerless over sin. Jesus often took issue with the Pharisees. He was usually harsh with them, but His admonition to them contains some good advice to all of us.

> *"Woe to you teachers of the law and Pharisees, you hypocrites! You clean the outside of the cup and dish, but inside they are full of greed and self-indulgence. Blind Pharisee! First clean the inside of the cup and dish, and then the outside also will be clean."*
> *(Matthew 23:25–26 NIV)*

Just in case we didn't really catch the message of looking at and dealing with the ugly things we all carry around inside of us, Jesus repeated the same message in a slightly different way.

> *"Woe to you teachers of the law and Pharisees, you hypocrites! You are like whitewashed tombs, which look beautiful on the outside but on the inside are full of dead men's bones and everything unclean. In the same way, on the outside you appear to people as righteous but on the inside you are full of hypocrisy and wickedness."*
> *(Matthew 23:27–28 NIV)*

Did you ever wonder where the phrase "skeletons in your closet" came from? Could it be that it was derived from this verse? Skeletons don't necessarily go away when you bring them out, but once you've aired them out, they tend to smell a lot better and become much easier to live with. Maybe the reason people can smell hypocrisy from a mile away is because of the stink of things we leave buried inside ourselves to rot, while asking them to come clean with theirs.

Many of us carry around secrets and we are sure if anyone found out what is really inside of us, they wouldn't love us anymore. We often tend to think "I'm the only person with such secrets, and because I have them, it is difficult to love myself." Of course some people have darker secrets than others, but we all have something we can take a little better look at. It is so interesting to see recovering addicts and long time Christians come together and discover that yes they do have differences in what they have been through, yet they have a lot of similar thoughts and experiences as well.

My psychologist has often accused me of "terminal uniqueness." What she means is, I am so sure my thoughts and feelings are so different from other people's, that it will keep me isolated and stop me from reaching out for the help and fellowship of other people. Certainly other people won't understand these strange and "unique" feelings, so I must keep them all inside where they rot. It has been very freeing to first learn through twelve step programs, that other recovering addicts have similar thoughts and feelings and then to find out through a small group in church that other so called "normal" Christian people have similar thoughts and feelings as well.

This made me feel part of the human race. It created a sense of belonging which in turn made it easier to get involved in my church. Were it not for these brave Christians with non-addictive backgrounds willingness to subject themselves to the twelve step process and be honest about their thoughts and feelings, I would have missed the important step in recovery of becoming part of a Christian church. These are the very people that have made me feel as if I have come home. They have made me feel welcome, a part of the church. I am eternally grateful that they took the time to understand me, instead of shying away because they didn't understand my past and therefore were a little afraid of me, or, worse yet, projecting an attitude that they were better than me. Words cannot express how wonderful it is, after all these years, to have a church home that fits. This is a feeling I want others to experience.

At the same time these caring, compassionate Christians have gained a better understanding of themselves. Many of the people in our small group twelve step Bible study have expressed they feel better about things in their past. Things like the death of a loved one, a relative with mental illness, someone in their family with an addiction problem or the struggle involved in the breakdown of a marriage. They have been honest about their own doubts and fears. We have discovered that we all have times we feel distant from God and doubts creep in. This is something that Christians don't always like to talk about; they want to be seen as solid, stable, unwavering Christians. It is so nice to find out that all Christians go through these times. It allows us to come out from behind our mask and relate with one another on an honest level. The willingness to share honestly on this level with yourself, God and others will be very rewarding for you. Carrying around feelings of fear that your different, resentment toward someone that has hurt you, the feeling of regret for treating others poor, not being able to extend or receive forgiveness, not making peace with a parent before they passed on, feeling like you should have been able to help someone that you couldn't, guilt, shame, feeling inadequate, wondering if you are really doing God's will, are things people at times keep all bottled up inside themselves. Keeping these things pushed down inside ourselves where we think others can't see them and carrying around all this stuff takes a lot of energy. It is also very stressful, the kind of stress that has been linked to many health problems.

The twelve step process, if approached in an honest manner, will help reduce the burden you carry. You will find you have more energy, better health and that you are able to relate more openly with others. It will also deepen and strengthen your relationship with God. Even if you start the twelve step journey purely to help yourself, as you move through the steps you will sense a deeper caring for others. You will want to reach out to those who still suffer. God always delights in our willingness to help others and always rewards it. You will develop more of the virtues Jesus modeled, virtues Paul wrote about in Colossians:

> *"Therefore, as God's chosen people, holy and dearly loved, clothe yourselves with compassion, kindness, humility, gentleness and patience. Bear with each other and forgive whatever grievances you have against one another. Forgive as the Lord forgave you. And over all these virtues put on love, which binds them all together in perfect unity."*
> *(Colossians 3:12–14 NIV)*

These are the types of things that don't smell from a mile away, traits that people will be drawn to. They are not that common in this world and people will want to get a closer look. As you acquire more of these virtues, you will become of great use to God in the lives of others. Your rewards will pile up in heaven. Because you took the time to better understand yourself through the twelve step process, you will be able to relate and share things about yourself with others, some of whom have suffered immeasurably. When you begin to relate with some of these people who so desperately need the healing power of Jesus in their life, you will become part of the miracle, something you will never tire of.

When you help others to see that even though we have our differences, we are not all that different, that we really are in the same boat, the boat that is sinking without Christ, you will help a person in need of a spiritual home, come home. This compassionate understanding and welcoming acceptance is perhaps the greatest gift you could give someone who has been pointed in the direction of God in one of the secular twelve step groups. To do this, you must see your own need for the healing power of God first.

As we go through the twelve steps in the following pages, try to begin applying them in your own life; you will be glad you did. But remember, it is not about perfection, it is about progress. This twelve step journey takes a lifetime, a very rewarding lifetime.

## 11. Trust God

The first three steps are about getting to a point where you trust God. First we find out we can't rely on ourselves, then we come to believe God can be relied on and thirdly we make a decision to turn our life over to God's care. If you are already there, you have a good start. It is, however, common to go back and forth on how much you turn over to God and how often you take control back. As we grow spiritually and learn more about ourselves we see new areas we need to turn over to God. For these reasons, we are never really done with the first three steps; in fact, they need to be done at least briefly every day, and we need to look more closely at them from time to time as well.

I find I have the best luck staying out of old behaviors if I turn my will and my day over to God each morning before getting out of bed. This custom is very well illustrated by a prayer a friend e-mailed a while back:

> "Dear Lord,
> So far today, I am doing all right. I have not gossiped, lost my temper, been greedy, grumpy, nasty, selfish, or self-indulgent. I have not whined, complained, cursed or eaten any chocolate. I have charged nothing on my credit card. But I will be getting out of bed in a min-

ute, and I think I will really need your help then."

The following poem of unknown origin, reminds us of the need to start our day by turning it over to God as well:

## THE DIFFERENCE

I got up early one morning and
rushed right into the day.
I had so much to accomplish that
I didn't have time to pray.
Problems just tumbled about me
and heavier came each task.
"Why doesn't God help me?" I wondered, He answered "You didn't ask."
I wanted to see joy and beauty, but the
day toiled on grey and bleak.
I wondered why God didn't show me,
He said "But you didn't seek."
I tried to come into God's presence;
I used all my keys at the lock.
God gently and lovingly chided
"My child you didn't knock."
I woke up early this morning, and
paused before entering the day,
I had so much to accomplish that
I had to take time to pray.

This is a lesson many addicts and alcoholics learn the hard way. After being sober for a while they slack off on their relationship with God and find themselves using once again. After more hard knocks, they once again hit bottom and come back to a twelve step meeting. When they say they don't understand their slip, someone inevitably will point out the following quote from the "Big Book" of Alcoholics Anonymous:

> "It is easy to let up on the spiritual program of action and rest on our laurels. We are headed for trouble if we do, for alcohol is a subtle foe. We are not cured of our alcoholism. What we really have is a daily reprieve contingent on the maintenance of our spiritual condition. Every day is a day when we must carry the vision of God's will into all of our activities. "How can I best serve Thee–Thy will (not mine) be done." These are thoughts that must go with us constantly. We can exercise our will along this line all we wish. It is the proper use of the will." (Alcoholics Anonymous, page 85)

Notice once again, if we replace the word alcohol with the word sin, and replace the word alcoholism with the words "sin nature," we are once again talking about our Christian walk, instead of alcoholism. The preceding paragraph points out the need for communication with God throughout the day. The best way to accomplish this is to start each day by turning ourselves over to the care of God. Let's look at each step more closely.

Step one says, "We admitted we were powerless over sin–that our lives had become unmanageable." Since I have an addictive personality, I sometimes wonder if I am headed into addiction with another behavior and ask my psychologist about it. She in turn asks me if it causes any unmanageability in my life. Is this behavior having negative consequences? Is it causing me to miss out on other things I should be doing? Is it causing me to hurt or neglect people? Is it affecting my relationship with God, myself or others? Am I in denial about some aspect of my behavior? Of course, because I am human, there is always some of this negativity in my life, this just points to the need to always realize I am powerless over my sin nature and the need to come back to step one often.

Denial is always what keeps us from taking step one. We say "It's not that big of a problem." "Everyone else does it and it doesn't seem to be hurting them." "Anyone in my circumstances would behave the same way." "If only my spouse would change, this wouldn't be a problem." "I still have my house, job and family, so my life can't be unmanageable." We will come up with all sorts of things to take the focus off potential problems in our lives. If you still tend to think the twelve steps are for alcoholics and they don't pertain to you, the following list of potential addictive agents, which is no where near complete, may help. The twelve steps can be applied to any one of them. This list comes from the introductory pages of a recovery Bible called "Serenity; A companion for twelve step recovery." It also contains the New Testament, Psalms and Proverbs with all of the verses pertaining to the twelve steps highlighted as well as comments about the various steps throughout.

---

1. Alcohol or drugs
2. Work, achievement, and success
3. Money addictions, such as overspending, gambling, hoarding
4. Control addictions, especially if they surface in personal, sexual, family, and business relationships
5. Food addictions
6. Sexual addictions
7. Approval dependency (the need to please people)
8. Rescuing patterns toward other persons
9. Dependency on toxic relationships (relationships that are damaging and hurtful)
10. Physical illness (hypochondria)
11. Exercise and physical conditioning
12. Cosmetics, clothes, cosmetic surgery, trying to look good on the outside
13. Academic pursuits and excessive intellectualizing
14. Religiosity or religious legalism (preoccupation with the form and the rules and regulations

of religion, rather than benefiting from the real spiritual message)
15. General perfectionism
16. Cleaning and avoiding contamination and other obsessive-compulsive symptoms
17. Organizing, structuring (the need always to have everything in it's place)
18. Materialism

(Serenity; A Companion for Twelve Step Recovery. Pages 13–14)

---

If you find yourself somewhere on this list don't be to hard on yourself; remember, we are all in the same boat and you can bet other people you know struggle with things on this list as well. The point is, you don't have to struggle with them. You can bring them out into the healing presence of Jesus Christ, but first you have to admit you need help. If looking deeper into some of these issues seems to overwhelm you, be comforted by knowing you only have to deal with things a little at a time, one day at a time. Just a willingness to start is all that's being asked. You have the rest of your life to work on these things. Whether you take some time to work on your issues or not, time will go by, so you may as well spend it doing something helpful and at the same time grow in your relationship with God.

Needing help is not something our society talks much about. We have been brought up to believe we can "reach down and pull ourselves up by our own bootstraps." If you have a problem, for Pete's sake don't ever talk about it; people will think you are weak. How often have you heard someone say, "We don't air our dirty laundry in public?" The truth is our society is built on pride and competition. If we tip our hand about potential problems, we have exposed weakness and will lose our competitive edge. Self-help books would have us believe that we can find the power to overcome and become whatever we want, if only we look deep enough into ourselves for the power and strength to do it.

We spoke earlier of raising the bottom by educating people to the fact that even though their lives have not yet been destroyed, when compared to those whose lives had been all but lost they are well on their way. Many people have had their lives destroyed by the behaviors on the list. Even if you are just starting to experience problems with any of these issues, take the word of those that have been there and start admitting your powerlessness now, instead of waiting for things to get unbearable.

The Bible contains many examples of people admitting they have problems they cannot overcome without bringing them to God. King David was a person that at times admitted utter defeat.

> *"My guilt has overwhelmed me like a burden to heavy to bear. My wounds fester and are loathsome because of my sinful folly. I am bowed down and brought very low; all day long I go about mourning."*
> *(Psalm 38:4–6 NIV)*

## *12 Steps* To a More Effective Christian Witness

Admitting you have a problem is the first step in resolving the problem. This is the essence of step one.

Step two is, "Came to believe that a power greater than ourselves could restore us to sanity." As a Christian, the concept of a power greater than you is an easy one, but do you believe that the almighty God cares and will help you through any problem you are having? Can you grasp the fact that the most powerful force in the universe wants a personal relationship with you, not only in the good times and in worship and praise for Him, but in your really bad times as well? He not only cares about your troubles, He is willing to go through them with you and give you what you need to heal, no matter how long it takes or how many times you need to start over. The Bible certainly indicates this is true.

> *"For He will deliver the needy who cry out, the afflicted who have no one to help. He will take pity on the weak and the needy and save the needy from death. He will rescue them from oppression and violence, for precious is their blood in His sight."*
> *(Psalm 72:12–14 NIV)*

> *"I have come into the world as a light, so that no one who believes in me should stay in darkness."*
> *(John 12:46 NIV)*

Jesus really does want to lead us out of the darkness in our lives. It is a matter of faith. How many times when healing someone did Jesus say it was their faith that healed them? Here again you need nothing like perfect faith to have God help you. Any amount of faith is enough to build on.

> *"I tell you the truth, if you have faith as small as a mustard seed, you can say to this mountain, "Move from here to there" and it will move. Nothing will be impossible for you."*
> (Matthew 17:21 NIV)

We can return to step two any time we want and build more faith. Sometimes what builds faith better than anything is moving on to step three and beginning to turn some stuff over to God. As you begin to see and feel results, your faith, like the mustard seed will grow.

Step three requires some action. "Made a decision to turn our will and our lives over to the care of God *as we understood Him.*" Not only do we make the decision to do it, we do it. This is not possible in the strictest sense. No matter how good of a job we do in turning our will and our lives over to God, our human nature will always take some of it back. The goal then becomes to leave a problem part of our life turned over just a little longer than we did last time.

This is a tall order! As human beings we have two big things in the way of doing this step. One is our self-centeredness tends to want what we want when we want it. The other, is our pride instills in us a desire to do it on our own. Because of these blocks, we need to practice turning everything over to God on a regular basis. Sometimes it will seem like a tennis match, with the ball in your court, then in God's court and then back to yours again. Do not be discouraged; any time the ball spends in God's court is helpful. The more you take things to Jesus in prayer, the more your faith and trust in God will grow. Even though you have already seen this prayer, this is the appropriate place for it. Pray it from time to time and you will become more able to trust God.

> "God I offer myself to Thee–to build with me and to do with me as Thou wilt. Relieve me of the bondage of self, that I may better do Thy will. Take away my difficulties, that victory over them may bear witness to those I would help of Thy Power, Thy Love, and thy way of life. May I do Thy will always!" (Alcoholics Anonymous, page 63)

## 12. Clean House

Once we have decided to trust God on as deep of a level as we can, it is time to take an honest and close look at our lives. Then we proceed by dealing with what we find. This can be a scary task and this is why it's important to bring God on board first. As we start going through cleaning ourselves up on the inside, we need to ask for God's help in doing so. Ask God to help you accurately look at yourself. Remember how powerful denial is. By asking God to help us take an honest look at ourselves, we will be capable of seeing how our life has gone and what problems need correcting. He will also help us get over the fear of really looking into those dark corners of our inner recesses.

Once we have a better look at ourselves, we can start to deal with what we find by talking about it with others and by being perfectly open with God. All of us have flaws that we can't help, but God can overcome them or put them to good use if we ask Him to. After all, God created us and knows our weaknesses and defects of character; He also knows our strengths and positive character traits. He knows just what to do with us because He has had a plan and a design for us all along. In order to come alongside of God's plan for us, we must be open about who we really are and what we have done or left undone, with ourselves, God and other people. As we go through this house cleaning, we will be able to unload the unnecessary burdens we carry around and we will see things we used to perceive as weaknesses, as strengths. God already accepts us how we are, we just need to get to the point where we can accept ourselves as we are. The next few steps will help to do just that.

This brings us to step four. "Made a searching and fearless moral inventory of ourselves." Many people have a very lengthy, written fourth step. One of the biggest things people do in drug and alcohol treatment centers is work on a fourth step; patients are expected to complete a fourth and fifth step before getting out. There are many fourth step guides available that will lead a person through in detail. Some people treat a fourth step as something you do once and then are done with. Other people in the twelve step community see it as an ongoing thing, something you work on the rest of your life. Granted, a person can include a lot and be very thorough their first time through and because of this thoroughness feel tremendous relief after following through with a fifth step, but there are always things one forgets. Then there are the cases where through the process of growth, you see a past behavior in a different light and need to go back to step four and add it to your inventory.

There are those that will say, "If you haven't done a written fourth step, you haven't done a fourth step." This is not necessarily true although writing some things down is a good start. Many people have explored past behavior or taken an inventory in the context of a counseling relationship. They have spent many sessions going through old behaviors and discussing hurtful behavioral problems. What is most important is that you catch the spirit of the fourth step, searching your past in an honest way to present a clear picture to yourself and who you are as well as where you've been. It is always a good idea, when going through past hurts and character defects to list the positive things about yourself as well; otherwise you will get a distorted picture. We all have done good deeds in our lives and contain many positive personality traits. Oddly enough, listing what's good about them is more difficult for many people than listing the bad. Peoples' self-esteem can get so low after years of living in darkness that they can't see the good. Other people see good traits in these people right off, but they can't see it in themselves, they need help and encouragement to find what is good in them.

If you need a catalyst to get started on an inventory of negative and hurtful things in your life, consider the "seven deadly sins." They are pride, greed, lust, anger, gluttony, envy, and sloth. Most people taking an honest inventory can see examples in their lives of at least one, if not all of these sins that are so very common to the human condition. This is not however an exercise in condemnation of people, it is an exercise to point out things that a person needs to make peace with, let go of, and turn over to God, so their burdens of guilt, shame and fear may be lightened.

Many of us have been hurt tremendously by the sins of others. This must be in our inventory as well. Some of these things such as childhood sexual abuse can be so very difficult to admit to being the victim of, but admitting how others have hurt us is necessary before we can begin to heal from these traumatic episodes. Many hurts from others have been more subtle, such as emotional abuse, or telling someone they are worthless or that they will never amount to anything. Sometimes the hurt just came from someone who should love you, ignoring you. Five things to list in conjunction with hurts caused by others are, who hurt me, how specifically did that person hurt me, what affect has it had on my life, what damage has it caused me and what was my part in it. This last one is so vitally important because in many cases people begin to believe they deserve to be abused and that somehow their behavior caused the abuse. It must be pointed out that this guilt is unrealistic, that the abused person needs to let themselves off the hook.

As you can see, a fourth step can go on at great length, but remember, us humans will never do it perfectly and the good news is you don't have to get it anywhere near perfect for it to start helping you. Just start with the obvious and as you go along ask God to reveal more about you, to you. Remember that recovery is a journey, not a destination.

In step five, we "admitted to God, to ourselves, and to another human being the exact nature of our wrongs." This means you admit all the stuff in your fourth step to God, go over it with yourself a few times and then share your fourth step with another human being. Once again, it is important to include your positive strengths and deeds as well; it will help the over all experience to be more productive.

Admitting our fourth step inventory to God is where we get the strength to complete the fifth step. First, it is so important to remember that God already knows all this stuff about you and loves you in spite of it. God will not reject you, He will rejoice in your openness. You can begin taking these things to God in prayer as you are doing your fourth step inventory. Many people find it helpful to go through the whole inventory all at once in prayer. Some people that have a hard time talking to God, or feel funny about talking to thin air about this stuff, have found it helpful to sit across from an empty chair, visualize God sitting in the chair, and then talk to God about it as if He were sitting right there. The ironic thing about this technique is that He is sitting right there. As you grow, you will have many opportunities to bring more up in prayer, so again don't worry about if you've included everything, just talk to God about whatever comes to mind.

As you have been doing all this inventory stuff and all this admitting to God, you have already begun the process of admitting it to yourself. As you go through this keep in mind, there is no sin God won't, through Jesus Christ, forgive. Give yourself a break; if God can forgive you, you can forgive yourself. This is also a process, not a single event, so just keep working on it.

Now we come to the part that is the most difficult to many people, admitting the exact nature of our wrongs to another person. The first real important thing is to find someone safe to do this with. Some suggestions would be a pastor, counselor, sponsor or accountability partner. It is necessary to go to someone that knows what a fifth step is and can be objective.

> "Do not give dogs what is sacred; do not through your pearls to pigs. If you do, they may trample them under their feet, and then turn and tear you to pieces."
> (Matthew 7:6 NIV)

This quote from Jesus shows us what can happen when we share information with just anyone. At best, they will drop it on the ground and walk on it. At worst, they will use this information to tear you to pieces. Generally it is not a good idea to do a fifth step with a spouse or close family member. They are too close to you, and too involved in the situation to be objective, and they could also be hurt by what you say. It is never all right for us to do anything in this house cleaning process that has the potential to hurt another person.

One of the benefits of sharing at this level with a safe person is you can find out firsthand you won't be rejected for your behavior; you can still relate to others even if they do know your deepest secrets.

Another benefit is the person you are sharing with will often tell you they have had some of the same thoughts, feelings and experiences. This will help you feel closer to the rest of humanity. Remember "terminal uniqueness"? It is always helpful to find out we are not that much different from others. These things help us feel more like a part of the human race.

After completing a fourth and fifth step you will begin to sense a great burden lifting off you. They are the beginning of putting down things you don't really need to carry in an emotional sense so you have room to start picking up more positive things. God can't fill you with love and peace if you are already full of junk. You have been able to deal with a lot of your past sin by just confessing it and asking forgiveness for it. What about things that go deeper, things that are more of a pattern, the underlying defects of character that have led to some of your poor behavior? This brings us to steps six and seven.

Step six says we "were entirely ready to have God remove all these defects of character." This seems somewhat strange at first; aren't we always ready to have our character defects removed? Strangely enough, the answer is often no. We have gotten rather used to some of these things. Even though they have caused trouble, they are familiar and we are afraid of what they may be replaced with. This is the basic fear of the unknown. We may also worry that along with getting rid of our character defects, we will lose the ability to have fun. Some people may believe they need some of their character defects to perform their job, an example being a used car salesman's need for the ability to stretch the truth just a little bit. This comes back to the first three steps in that it is a matter of trusting God. We must believe that whatever God replaces these character defects with will be good. The truth is, God will take you places you never dreamed possible. You will find fun on a new level. You will find that integrity is a great asset in the business world; if you treat someone fairly, you have created a customer for life. We need to trust that if we turn our wills and our lives, including all our character defects, over to the care of God, He will not let us down. The Bible says:

> *"My soul is weary with sorrow; strengthen me according to your word. Keep me from deceitful ways; be gracious to me through your law. I have chosen the way of truth; I have set my heart on your laws. I hold fast to your statutes, O Lord; do not let me be put to shame. I run in the path of your commands, for you have set my heart free. Teach me, O Lord, to follow your degrees; then I will keep them to the end. Give me understanding and I will keep your law and obey it with all my heart. Direct me in the path of your commands, for there I find delight. Turn my heart toward your statutes and not toward selfish gain. Turn my eyes away from worthless things; preserve my life according to your word."*
> *(Psalm 119:28–37 NIV)*

This passage asks God to change us, indicating we can't do it on our own. We can see throughout this passage that God will transform us and when we are on His path, we will find delight. Now that we have become ready to have God remove our character defects, it's time for step seven.

"Humbly asked Him to remove our shortcomings." The importance of humility is often talked about when discussing this step. Humility is simply realizing that I can't change these shortcomings on my own, but God can. Humility is the knowledge that God is all-powerful and that I am not. Once we know this, we have no use for false pride. Many people think that humility is a bad thing, a weakness. The truth is, coming humbly to God is a tremendous source of strength. This is also a step that bears repeating fairly often; we need to come humbly before God every day and he will gradually mold us.

Let's look at the step seven prayer you read in chapter six again:

> "My Creator, I am now willing that you should have all of me, good and bad. I pray that you now remove from me every single defect of character which stands in the way of my usefulness to you and my fellows. Grant me strength, as I go from here, to do your bidding. Amen." (Alcoholics Anonymous, page 76)

One of the cool things about this prayer is that it leaves which shortcomings to remove up to God. It is asking to have God remove the character defects that make us useless to Him or other people. As we grow with God and progress through the twelve steps, we become more "other centered." This is nothing to be afraid of. You will not lose yourself in this process, you will find your real self–you will find the person God intended for you to be. This is the best we can hope for in this world, and it will produce reasonable happiness, peace of mind and true fulfillment.

Throughout most of my life I have felt too ashamed of my character defects, the sin in my life, to speak openly with God about them. Much of the time this left little to talk to God about. It didn't seem right to talk to God about the character defects and sin in my life until I was ready to give them up and certain that I could follow through with giving them up. Steps six and seven have taught me to talk openly about the ongoing defects and sin in my life to God on a very regular basis, telling Him they are part of me and I don't know if I can give them up and asking Him to remove the things from me that He sees need to be removed. I don't pray for God to make me perfect so I can serve Him, I pray that God may find a way to make use of me in spite of my defects and sin nature. This doesn't mean I don't try to sin less, for I know that the less I sin, the better off I will be because I will have less of the consequences of sin to deal with. What it does mean is that to some degree I am sure I will always sin as long as I am a part of this imperfect world and that I believe God will make use of me in spite of this ongoing sin.

If God had an army consisting of only perfect

human soldiers, it would be a small one. Who could be better than God, the being that created you and knows every detail about you, to talk openly with about your ongoing shortcomings, character defects and sin? By dealing with the shame and guilt that arises from not being perfect directly with God in prayer, and accepting this imperfection in yourself realizing that God has already accepted it, you make yourself more available for service to God.

## 13. Give and Receive Forgiveness

Steps eight and nine are about mending our relationships with people. We were created to have relationships with other people. Perhaps you have heard the saying "No man is an island." We can all think of examples of people who have isolated themselves from society, but they are not emotionally healthy people. God tells us right off the bat in the Bible that it's not good to be alone:

> *"The Lord God said, 'It is not good for the man to be alone. I will make a helper suitable for him.'"*
> *(Genesis 2:18 NIV)*

Some people have had such bad experiences with people, both in what they have done to others and what others have done to them, that they have walled themselves off from other people. They may be around other people and even interact with other people, yet because of resentment, bitterness, guilt and shame they feel alone. This kind of loneliness cannot be overcome without the help of God and an examination of their relationships with people. Even if you do relate well and connect with others, we have all hurt someone and have all been hurt by someone. Everyone has something to gain from working these steps.

Step eight says, "Made a list of all persons we have harmed, and became willing to make amends to them all." We already have a start to the first part of this step in our fourth step inventory. Any person you admitted to harming in the fourth and fifth steps belongs here. As you think further about those you have harmed, look closely at your family of origin, your children, your spouse and your spouse's family. Consider the community of people at your job, your neighborhood, or in your church. As you are thinking about what you have done to people, think also about what you have left undone that you should have done. Oftentimes our sins are sins of omission.

It may seem as though to do this will only dredge up more guilt and shame. Some of these things have been put behind you, why stir them up, after all, you can't change the past, what's done is done. The truth is that by going through with these steps you will vastly reduce the amount of shame and guilt you feel and carry. Even if you believe you have put some of this past behavior toward people neatly away somewhere, it is still with you causing a negative drain on your ability to live as God would have you live unless you become willing to make amends for it. This is how Jesus responds to those that are willing to make amends:

> *"But Zacchaeus stood up and said to the lord, 'Look, Lord! Here and now I give half my possessions to the poor, and if I have cheated anybody out of anything, I*

> *will pay back four times the amount.' Jesus said to him, 'Today salvation has come to this house.'"*
>
> *(Luke 19:8–9 NIV)*

Your willingness to make amends starts by asking God to help you become willing. It is also beneficial to hear others share how much more at peace they are after doing so. You also have to want more room for God in your life; making amends makes more room for God. The willingness may not come all at once, in fact it probably won't. The important thing is that you start, in prayer, to become willing. Once you have made this start, it will grow like a snowball rolling down a hill. Every journey starts with one step.

Step nine reports that we "made direct amends to such people wherever possible, except when to do so would injure them or others." As our willingness from step eight grows, the opportunity to make some of these amends will present itself. As it does, we make them. Sometimes you have to go out of your way to make amends with someone you wouldn't normally run into. Do it. You must realize however, that just because we are ready to make amends doesn't mean the person we are making them to is ready to hear them. In these cases it is important that you not feel like you have failed in your amends. You are responsible for the effort, not the result. A sincere apology, whether accepted or not will unload the burden you carry about it. Often though, your amends will fall on receptive ears and it can be a very rewarding experience that rekindles a relationship once strained by old behaviors. Jesus said:

> *"Therefore, if you are offering your gift at the altar and there remember your brother has something against you, leave your gift there in front of the altar. First go and be reconciled to your brother; then come and offer your gift."*
> *(Matthew 5:23–24 NIV)*

The last part of this step is important to touch on as well. How could making amends to someone injure them or others? The classic case would be if someone had been unfaithful with another man's wife and the other man never knew about it. If amends were made directly to this person, he would obviously be upset. This could also trickle down and hurt innocent children. Sometimes someone has caused such a traumatic experience in the life of another, just meeting up with them again would be too painful. If our amends could hurt someone in any way, we find another way to make them. In cases like these, you can write a letter of apology to the person, but never mail it. Some people find it therapeutic to burn it and let the smoke carry away the burden of guilt they bear. This is a good time to make use of a sponsor or accountability partner. It would be too easy for us to put many of our amends in this category just so we don't have to make them. A good sponsor will tell you if you are avoiding making amends to protect someone else from being hurt or if you are just trying to get out of doing it to save yourself from an uncomfortable situation.

You may be wondering by now what these steps have to do with forgiveness. Granted, when making amends we are asking for forgiveness, but where does forgiving others enter in? The truth is, we cannot ask for forgiveness without offering forgiveness. They go together. Jesus said:

> *"Do not judge and you will not be judged. Do not condemn and you will not be condemned. Forgive, and you will be forgiven. Give, and it will be given to you. A good measure, pressed down, shaken together and running over, will be poured into your lap. For with the measure you use, it will be measured to you."*
> *(Luke 6:37–38 NIV)*

Forgiveness is the most important message of the New Testament. God knows that nothing good can be built on top of sin, so in order to be able to do anything with us powerless sinful humans; He had to provide a way for us to be forgiven. It is so important that He sent His son to die so we could be forgiven. Asking God for forgiveness is the place to start. We will not be able to adequately give and receive forgiveness to others without squaring things with God. We have already started the process of admitting our faults to God in the previous steps. This is something we need to continue. Confess specific things in prayer when they are on your mind, and ask God in a general way to forgive all your sins. Sometimes the more difficult thing here is to actually feel like you are forgiven. This takes us back to building trust in God. You need to have a certain measure of faith before you can start to feel forgiven. Faith comes from doing and then seeing the results. The more you seek forgiveness from God, the more forgiven you will feel.

Many people have worked on the making of amends for a long time without ever thinking about making amends to themselves. This can be tough. We are quite often our own worst critic. This seems like a small point, but in the life of many twelve steppers, it's the one thing that is missing. They have gone through with their lists, they have made amends and restitution to every person they run into. They just haven't let themselves off the hook. Ask yourself, have I really extended forgiveness to myself? Have I been able to accept myself just as I am, the way that God accepts me? If not, ask yourself, if God can forgive me and others can forgive me, why don't I forgive myself?

Oftentimes, the guilt people can't seem to let go of is unrealistic. They blame themselves for things others were responsible for. Sometimes when people have been abused or mistreated by another person, they can't figure out why the other person is doing this to them. This causes them to believe it must be because of something bad they did and therefore they deserve to be treated poorly. This attitude is more common than you may think. The big problem with forgiving yourself for this kind of guilt is even though you've convinced yourself you did something bad to deserve this treatment, you don't really know what it was. As long as you look inside yourself for the reason, you will never find it because the reason for someone else's behavior is in them.

Once they see that they didn't do anything to cause the other person's behavior, they can begin to let go of the unrealistic guilt. The next thing these people need to do if they truly want to be free of what happened to them is to forgive the person that hurt them. It seems almost cruel to ask someone that has been molested as a child, someone that has been beaten for years by their spouse, or someone that has been raped to forgive their attacker. You may think these are evil people that don't deserve forgiveness. Actually, forgiving a person has absolutely nothing to do with whether or not they deserve to be forgiven or even whether or not they are asking to be forgiven. It has to do with the forgiver, not the forgiven. It is the only way to unload the anger, resentment, and bitterness the victim is carrying around.

Another example of a person that needs to forgive someone but it almost seems wrong to forgive them, is a person that has lost a child. Consider the case of a person whose young adult daughter, with her whole life ahead of her, has been abducted, raped, tortured and killed. You would hardly blame this person for being angry, bitter, resentful or even for feeling like killing the attacker themselves. This is a horrific situation, but the sad fact is, that person will never have a moment of true peace as long as they carry this anger and resentment around with them. The only way they can unload this burden is by forgiving the attacker.

You may say this is impossible. It is not impossible if the person seeks God's help. The method of getting rid of a resentment toward another that is often recommended in twelve steps groups is that of praying that God will bless the life of the person you have a resentment towards, everyday for two weeks. Magically, at the end of this time it will be gone. In less severe cases it really works in that time period; however, my own personal experience tells me that in some cases it takes considerably longer.

After my divorce and the loss of my intact family, I had tremendous resentment and anger toward my ex-wife and her new boyfriend for whom she left me. I had fantasies of burning down their house, with them in it, but I figured I would be the first suspect and I don't much care for jail. I was torn apart with grief. I had never been so hurt in all my life. When people in the divorce support group I was going to recommended I forgive her and wish her well, I was certain they didn't understand how badly I was hurting. With hindsight, I now see that they did understand how badly I was hurting and that's precisely why they wanted me to forgive her. They knew forgiveness was the only road to peace and healing for me. So I started to pray everyday that God would bless her and her new boyfriend. God knew I didn't mean it; I was seething with anger and hate underneath the words. I kept on praying for them and kept on not meaning it. One day I realized that something had changed; I really did mean it and realized I did still care about her and that I did wish her well. It was at that moment that I first had complete peace about it and it only took five years of praying without really meaning it to get there. I truly believe, had I not done that, I would still be filled with bitterness and resentment.

As humans, our forgiveness is never perfect or complete. We may mean it for a while and then take it back. When God forgives, He forgets; the slate is wiped clean. Often, we have to forgive the same thing or that same person over and over. Some people wonder how many times are enough. The answer is, how ever many times it takes. You may be thinking that five years to truly forgive someone is too long to keep at it. Jesus said:

> *"At that point Peter got up the nerve to ask, 'Master, how many times to I forgive a brother or sister who hurts me? Seven?'*
> *Jesus replied, 'Hardly, try seventy times seven.'"*
> *(Matthew 18:21 22 MES)*

I once heard resentment compared to a snake bite. You can never get un-bitten, however, it's not the bite of a snake that kills you, it's the spread of the venom, and you can stop the spread of the venom. When a person has injured you, you can't have the injury taken back, but you can stop the deadly spread of resentment. When we hold resentment against someone, it is like us taking poison and expecting the person we resent to get sick. Forgiveness is our road to peace of mind. Jesus tells us:

> *"But I tell you who hear me: Love your enemies, do good to those who hate you, bless those who curse you, pray for those who mistreat you."*
> *(Luke 6:27–28 NIV)*

This is all very difficult to do, but it is not without rewards. After explaining steps one through nine, the "Big Book" of Alcoholics Anonymous tells of some of the benefits that come from working these steps. They are referred to in AA as "the promises" and are often the topic for a meeting. They apply to anyone working the twelve steps, not just alcoholics.

"If we are painstaking about this phase of our development, we will be amazed before we are half way through. We are going to know a new freedom and a new happiness. We will not regret the past nor wish to shut the door on it. We will comprehend the word serenity and we will know peace. No matter how far down the scale we have gone, we will see how our experience can benefit others. That feeling of uselessness and self-pity will disappear. We will lose interest in selfish things and gain interest in our fellows. Self-seeking will slip away. Our whole attitude and outlook upon life will change. Fear of people and of economic insecurity will leave us. We will intuitively know how to handle situations which used to baffle us. We will suddenly realize that God is doing for us what we could not do for ourselves.

Are these extravagant promises? We think not. They are being fulfilled among us—sometimes quickly, sometimes slowly. They will always materialize if we work for them." (Alcoholics Anonymous pages 83–84)

## 14. Help Others

The last three steps are often referred to as the maintenance steps. They remind us to continue looking at ourselves and working on our spiritual growth on a daily basis. Even though the only real mention of helping others is in the last part of the last step, all of the last three steps are important in helping others. Once you have gone through the first nine, you have gained some insight that you can share with those who still suffer. You will still want to revisit these first nine steps from time to time. As you grow in the Lord and gain new insight and understanding, there will be more work to do in the first nine steps. In order to be an effective witness for Christ, you need to add a commitment of continued growth to the foundation you have already laid.

Remember, our example is our most powerful form of witness. In order to attract others to Christ, our lives must appear attractive. Nothing is more attractive to a hurting person than a person that appears to have a deep peace and satisfaction in their life. This peace and satisfaction can only come from sustained growth in our relationship with Jesus Christ. Constant working of steps ten through twelve will assure continuous spiritual growth.

Step ten says, "Continued to take personal inventory and when we were wrong promptly admitted it."

*12 Steps*
TO A MORE EFFECTIVE CHRISTIAN WITNESS

The Bible says:

*"Be diligent in these matters; give yourself wholly to them, so that everyone may see your progress. Watch your life and doctrine closely. Persevere in them, because if you do, you will save both yourself and your hearers."*
*(1 Timothy 4:15–16 NIV)*

We will all make mistakes, sin if you prefer, the rest of our lives. It is unreasonable for people to expect otherwise, even for Christians. What people do notice about, and expect from Christians, is how fast they admit and rectify those mistakes. When we don't promptly confess and set right our sin, we are in obvious opposition to what Jesus stands for and therefore are not a very good walking billboard for Christianity. Of course, by not promptly admitting our mistakes, we also jeopardize that all so wonderful peace of mind that God has given us.

Many people go back to step three in prayer every morning, turning their will and their life over to God for the day. In their evening prayers, before retiring for the day, they consider step ten. Oftentimes twelve steppers will have some disagreement over what belongs in step ten and what belongs in step four. It doesn't really matter as long as they end up in one or the other. Most would say that if you confess your sin in the day you commit it, it goes in your tenth step daily inventory. If your offense goes longer, perhaps you will need to back up to step four and once again do a more thorough inventory.

Remember; always look for positive things in your inventory as well as the negative. This can be your progress check. If you have had many positive and peaceful moments in your day, acknowledge them and then thank God for them. Moments of peace and positive accomplishment are a gift from God.

Step eleven is the real meat of the twelve step program. All of the steps have been moving us along to a closer relationship with God. Many people, even Christians, have a hard time believing that God wants to be involved and has the time as well as resources to be involved in every aspect of our lives. Although none of us will ever be able to let God in completely, step eleven works us toward that goal by saying we "sought through prayer and meditation to improve our conscious contact with God, *as we understood Him,* Praying only for knowledge of His will for us and the power to carry that out."

Many people in twelve step situations have not had much exposure to prayer, and to them meditation sounds like some mysterious eastern discipline. They worry that even if they did decide to give it a try, they would do it wrong. Prayer and meditation are really very simple, and the only wrong way to do it is to not do it at all! Prayer is talking to God, meditation is listening to God. There are many formal prayers that we can repeat either out loud or to ourselves; God will always hear the silent voice in our mind. The real neat time that comes in a person's prayer life, is when they use the silent voice in their mind to just talk to God in their normal way of talking and they feel free to talk about anything. God wants to hear what we are anxious about, what we are exited about, what we fear we have done wrong and what we have done right. He wants us to involve Him in everything.

Meditation, or listening for God's communication to us, can also be done in as many different ways as there are people to do it. Usually it involves creating a quite time when you can still your mind and just sit and wait for God to put something into your mind. Many people find it easiest to meditate when surrounded by nature, things that God made. Some find sitting and watching an animal helpful. For others, just a quite room or soft instrumental music does the trick. One mother of several children made it known to her children that when she sat down and flipped her apron over her head, she was meditating and it would be unwise to interrupt her. Find whatever works for you, a way you can quiet your mind and just open your heart and soul to God. It is also very possible to hear God during the course of your day by simply turning your thoughts toward Him.

After practicing the eleventh step awhile you will find yourself in communication with God throughout the day. I am often in direct conversation with God as I am going about my daily chores. The conversation really does go both ways and sometimes God speaks first, usually about some impatient little fit or self-centered thought I am having and I just say, "I know God, you're right." Other times I am actively seeking His will for my life. I learned long ago that my self-centered will just leads to misery and that more of the same (my self-will) will bring more of the same (misery). I also know that God's will is going to be much better than anything I would think possible; He has already proven that to me. I am excited to see where God is leading me. He gives me glimpses of where I'm going, but not details. He wants me to trust Him to work things out.

 You can get to a point of frequent contact with God just by trying to think of Him a little more today than you did yesterday. It also helps if you are not hanging on so tightly to your own will. As the step said, we are to pray only for knowledge of His will for us and the power to carry it out. Some of us are used to asking God for specific things we think we want. God knows what we really want more than we do. If it is your habit to pray about specific things, whether for yourself or for others, you can bring it in line with the spirit of step eleven by simply tacking "if it's Your will" on the end. The best prayer you can ever pray for others is that God finds a way to work His will in their life. It is also the best prayer you can pray for yourself. The Bible says:

> *"Meanwhile, the moment we get tiered in the waiting, God's spirit is right alongside helping us along. If we don't know how or what to pray, it doesn't matter. He does our praying in and for us, making prayer out of*

*our wordless sighs, our aching groans. He knows us far better than we know ourselves, knows our pregnant condition, and keeps us present before God. That's why we can be so sure that every detail in our lives for God is worked into something good."*
*(Romans 8:26–28 MES)*

The main thing in improving our conscious contact with God is that we think about Him more. If we turn our mind and heart in His direction, the rest will come. As we pray for knowledge of God's will for us, we ought not to be surprised when it has something to do with helping others by spreading the message and love of God to them. Remember, this is why God leaves us here once we are saved instead of taking us straight home to Heaven.

This brings us to step twelve, "Having had a spiritual awakening as a result of these steps, we tried to carry this message to others, and to practice these principles in all our affairs." When people share how grateful they are for the darkness in their life that brought them to a twelve step program, it doesn't mean the problem in their life was not that bad or that they would ever wish it on anyone else, it just means they are afraid, were it not for the great difficulties in their life, they would have never had this spiritual awakening. The goal of the twelve steps is not to eradicate whatever dark behavior you bring into it. Doing away with the behavior is a starting point. The goal is an ever increasing spiritual awakening and they knew whatever price they paid to get there was worth it.

Once we have had this spiritual awakening, it needs to be evident in all our affairs. The principles we have learned have to spill over into every aspect of our life. Paul wrote:

> *"But what happens when we live God's way? He brings gifts into our lives, much in the same way that fruit appears in an orchard–things like affection for others, exuberance about life, serenity. We develop a willingness to stick with things, a sense of compassion in the heart, and a conviction that a basic holiness permeates things and people. We find ourselves involved in loyal commitments, not needing to force our way in life, able to marshal and direct our energies wisely.*
>
> *Legalism is helpless in bringing this about; it only gets in the way. Among those who belong to Christ, everything connected with getting our own way and mindlessly responding to what everyone else calls necessities is killed off for good–crucified.*
>
> *Since this is the kind of life we have chosen, the life of the spirit, let us make sure that we do not just hold it as an idea in our heads or a sentiment in our hearts, but work out its implications in every detail of our lives.*

*That means we will not compare ourselves with each other as if one of us were better and another worse. We have far more interesting things to do with our lives. Each of us is an original."*
*(Galatians 5: 22–26 MES)*

Again, none of us are anywhere near perfectly reflecting this passage, but we are making great progress toward it. If we live our lives in the care of Christ, it should be evident in our lives. As these characteristics develop in our lives, taking this message to those who still suffer becomes a bigger part of our lives. We have gone through a large amount of looking inward. This is a very important part of developing our Christian witness, but now, not only will we continue to look at ourselves, we will take this message to whom ever God puts in our path who needs the healing, guidance and compassion of Jesus Christ. We will love whom ever God puts in front of us.

*"All praise to the God and Father of our Master, Jesus the Messiah! Father of all mercy! God of all healing counsel! He comes alongside us when we go through hard times, and before you know it, He brings us alongside someone else who is going through hard times so that we can be there for that person just as God was there for us. We have plenty of hard times that*

*come from following the Messiah, but no more so than the good times of His healing comfort–we get a full measure of that too."*
*(2 Corinthians 1:3–5 MES)*

With this thought in mind, the rest of this book will examine the ins and outs of working with those who still suffer. If we let Him, God will bring us alongside someone that is going through hard times and we will find that in doing so, we not only gain deeper appreciation for those around us, we will grow closer to God. Spiritual growth is mostly about being of service to others.

## 15. Attract Others to Christ

Many times in our excitement and enthusiasm for Christ, we think everyone should have a relationship with Jesus, and therefore can come on kind of strong. We try to push God on people. Of course, reaching everyone with the good news of Jesus is the goal, but when most people feel pushed, they dig in their heels. When it comes to talking about God, many people's guards are already up, and if they sense any forcefulness at all, they look for the first chance to escape from your presence and write you off as a religious fanatic. This brings to mind the old saying "you can't push a wet noodle through mud." When you think about it, it's true, a wet noodle is far to limp and when you try to push it, it's going to bend in whatever way is easiest, and if you keep pushing it you will go right on by the noodle. On the other hand, you can pull it or attract it toward you and it will follow. You make much better progress if you lead the noodle through the mud.

So it is with our Christian witness. We need to first look at ourselves and make sure that we practice what we preach. We must be honest about the closeness of our own relationship with God. Am I receiving enough from God in my life, so it is obvious to those around me that I have something as wonderful as what I am telling them they could have? We must attract people to Christ, not push them. We must lead by example. Paul, in his letter to Titus said:

> *"But mostly, show them this by doing it yourself, incorruptible in your teaching, your words solid and sane. Then anyone who is dead set against us, when he finds nothing weird or misguided, might eventually come around.*
>
> *Guide slaves into being loyal workers, a bonus to their masters–no back talk, no petty thievery. Then their good character will shine through their actions, adding luster to the teaching of our savior God."*
> (Titus 2:7–10 MES)

It is not being suggested that we never bring up the subject of God in our lives out in the world, just that we don't go overboard. If someone asks how your weekend was, tell them a little about it including something about church. Maybe this will lead to an opportunity to invite them to church. If it does, do so, but then leave it there. If you dog them all week about it, they are not likely to come; they will already be sick of hearing about church, so why would they actually show up for more. Oftentimes we are just responsible to plant a seed; God will make the seed grow. Something that you say or do now, even though it didn't get someone to church, may have started a thought process that will eventually lead them to church.

There is a delicate balance between saying too

little and saying too much. Exactly where that line is differs from person to person. As you speak of God, gauge the reaction of the person you are talking to. If they appear interested or start asking questions, keep going. If they seem disinterested or turned off by your talking about God, back off and give the seed time to grow. From time to time it may be appropriate to plant a new seed if it appears that the first one fell on rocky ground. Jesus explains how some seeds flourish and others don't in the following parable:

> *"A farmer went out to sow his seed. As he was scattering the seed, some fell along the path, and the birds came and ate it up. Some fell on rocky places, where it did not have much soil. It sprang up quickly, because the soil was so shallow. But when the sun came up, the plants were scourged, and they withered because they had no root. Other seed fell among thorns, which grew up and choked the plants. Still other seed fell on good soil, where it produced a crop– a hundred, sixty or thirty times what was sown. He, who has ears, let them hear."*
> (Matthew 13:3 9 NIV)

Does this mean that if someone seems to be rocky soil or a weed patch we just give up? No, it just offers an explanation to why the seed didn't do well. When farmers find a place in their field where the soil is too rocky or thin, they try to build the soil up by adding organic matter, manure or fertilizer. If they find a patch of weeds, they do something to eradicate the weeds so they may have better luck next year. A good farmer takes note of why his crop did poorly and makes adjustments for it.

Maybe the person who seems like rocky soil needs more time. Your continued example of a life full of love, peace, kindness and fulfillment may be the manure needed to build up this person's soil to where it can sustain a crop. Sometimes the weeds may be the other people around the person you have been trying to witness to. Perhaps you will do better if you wait for a chance to catch this person away from these weeds. People can be far more accessible when they don't have to worry about what their peers may think.

Another unattractive thing that Christians sometimes do is to isolate themselves with people of similar belief. It is good to fellowship with other believers and sometimes the secular crowd is uncomfortable for Christians to be around, but it leaves an impression with other people that you think you are superior to them. With this separation, you will not have a chance to model the wonders Christ has done in your life, and certainly no one is going to be asking you things like, "How is it that you always seem so upbeat and positive, isn't life a dismal existence for everyone?" To be attractive to those that don't know the Lord, you have to be around them. The Bible says:

> *"Bless those who persecute you; bless and do not curse. Rejoice with those who rejoice; mourn with those who mourn. Live in harmony with one another. Do not be proud, but be willing to associate with people of low position. Do not be conceited."*
> *(Romans 12:14–16 NIV)*

In other words, be friendly to those in need of Christ's love. Your friendliness may be just the fertilizer their rocky soil needs to become fertile enough to sustain a crop. If you get some ribbing from time to time about being churchy or religious or a whole host of other expressions that are sometimes directed at Christians, even though it can be hurtful, bless them by just leaving it lie and still associating with them. Hurting people can be hard, like the path from which the birds stole the seed. They make hurtful remarks to others simply because, "Hurt people, hurt people." Maybe your willingness to let the little remarks go and still be friendly is the spade which will loosen the hard-packed soil just enough to cover the seed and protect it from the birds.

Have some fun in your life. Real fun is attractive. If you are not currently getting together with others in your church to just have fun from time to time, start doing so. Once you do, you will have some lighter stuff to share with people about your weekend. Then start to invite people from outside the church to the fun activities. One of the reasons people resist God and the church is because they are afraid if they come to God they will never have fun again. The truth is they aren't really having fun with the behaviors they are caught up in anyway. They talk as if the party they went to was great fun when they were around their "weed" buddies, when in reality, they don't remember if they had fun or not and spent a good share of the evening with their head in the toilet saying "Never again." Of course, as with all addictions, most likely they will do it again rather soon. If we as Christians seem a little less like a stick in the mud, and offer them hope of having some real fun, it may attract them and it is very good for us as well.

Last fall our church got together for a hayride, and all it took was someone with a wagon and tractor. Afterwards, we built a fire and roasted hotdogs. Then the pastor brought out his guitar and we sat around the camp fire singing old songs. They weren't even religious songs; they were songs from our teen years. (We lost the younger crowd on a couple of them.) Everyone still talks about it months later and you can bet most of them have talked to people they met in their everyday lives about how fun it was. Next year we will probably need two wagons.

As a child, our Luther League went on a couple of five day canoe trips. They were a lot of fun at the time. They were thirty five years ago and I still remember them fondly. Over the years, whenever the subject of canoeing came up, I shared with others the fun we had in that church group. Just recounting an old memory of something fun can plant a seed for someone afraid of never having fun in the church.

There are countless things you can do with your church as a whole or in smaller groups. Some other examples might be game night, movie night, or sports that are for fun instead of competition like bad mitten or volleyball. Roller-skating provides some fond childhood church group memories as well. If you are not having fun in your church setting now, start having fun. Once you are having fun, don't be afraid to talk about the fun you had at church with the people in your everyday life. You would be surprised how deep of a longing many people have to be involved in this kind of thing, but they can't always admit it, especially around the weeds. You may also be surprised to find out how much of a longing you have to do these things. Nowhere in the Bible does it say Christians can't ever have fun.

Once you have some fun activities, invite people from outside the church that show any interest. One suggestion for inviting people from the twelve step community to your church events is by leaving flyers for them that specifically invite them. Many churches have an "in" with these groups because they often rent space for their meetings from churches. Just leave the flyers in the room you know they have their meeting in. Once they start coming to some events, you have a lot more time away from the weeds to have conversations with this person about things that may be hurting them and more chances to tell how God will heal people's hurts. Maybe when change starts to take place in the life of this person, some of the weeds will show interest and start coming. One thing that Jesus can do that the farmer can't do, is turn the weeds into a desirable plant. He does this by grafting the wild plant onto His root:

> *"Behind and underneath all this there is a holy, God-planted, God tended root. If the primary root of the tree is holy, there's bound to be some holy fruit. Some of the trees branches were pruned and you wild olive shoots were grafted in. Yet the fact that you are now fed by that rich and holy root gives you no cause to crow over the pruned branches. Remember, you aren't feeding the root, the root is feeding you."*
> *(Romans 11:16–18 MES)*

Your example is what makes being grafted in to the root of Christ attractive or unattractive to those who still suffer. Be sure that you exhibit an example that is peaceful, fun loving, friendly, caring, and compassionate, one that says you don't feel you are too good to associate with them, and some people will be attracted to Christ through you. A graft into the root of Christ does not have to resemble a stick in the mud!

## 16. Some People Fear the Church

Even though we have done what we can to make a relationship with God attractive, many people will still seam hesitant and shy away. One of the reasons they shy away is somewhere they have picked up a negative attitude toward the church. It is important to realize this so you can project a certain amount of understanding when their negative feelings come up. Of course, like with anything, negative emotions are often based on some kind of fear.

I know from personal experience that some people pick up the message of fear from church itself. Not only did I get a certain amount of "You better watch out or God will get you" influence from my family while growing up, it was taught in the church as well. People in the church often spoke of the need to fear God. The expression "God-fearing Christian" was a common one. While going through confirmation in the Lutheran church, we spent a lot of time studying Martian Luther's explanations of the Ten Commandments, the Apostles' Creed and the Lord's Prayer. If memory serves me right, most, if not all of his explanations started with the phrase, "We are to fear and love God." This always seemed contradictory to me. In Sunday school we had learned much about a God who is loving and caring, a God that took care of the birds and flowers and encouraged little children to come to Him.

> *"Look at the birds of the air, they do not sow or reap or store away in barns, and yet your Heavenly Father feeds them. Are you not much more valuable than they? Who of you by worrying can add a single hour to his life?*
> *And why do you worry about clothes? See how the lilies of the field grow. They do not labor or spin. Yet I tell you not even Solomon in all his splendor was dressed like one of these. If that is how God clothes the grass of the field, which is here today and tomorrow is thrown into the fire, will He not much more clothe you, oh you of little faith."*
> *(Matthew 6:26–30 NIV)*

> *"The people brought children to Jesus, hoping He might touch them. The disciples shooed them off. But Jesus was irate and let them know it: 'Don't push these children away. Don't ever get between them and me. These children are at the very center of life in the kingdom. Mark this: Unless you accept God's kingdom in the simplicity of a child, you'll never get in.' Then gathering up the children in His arms, he laid his hands of blessing on them."*
> *(Mark 10:13–16 MES)*

It sure seemed to me that there was no need to

fear a God that encouraged us not to worry, blessed the little children and told us that the road to heaven is a simple affair that children can easily grasp. Yet this fear thing persists, often used as a tool to get children to do what an adult wants them to do. Sometimes they back up this need to be afraid with some Old Testament story of God's wrath.

> *"Then God rained brimstone and fire down on Sodom and Gomorrah–a river of lava from God out of the sky!—and destroyed these cities and the entire plain and everyone who lived in the cities and everything that grew from the ground. But Lot's wife looked back and turned into a pillar of salt."*
> *(Genesis 19:24–26 MES)*

Well I sure didn't want to get caught up in one of these fire and brimstone events, and turning to a pillar of salt didn't seem like a good idea either. So this was the start of a major conflict in my spiritual life, a conflict that was partially responsible for keeping me pressed down in the darkness and despair of drug and alcohol abuse for sixteen years, after I first realized I had a desperate problem and seriously wanted to quit. I still carried with me the idea that God loved me and would help and many times asked for His help, but I also had this fear that kept me from looking God's way for help once I started to screw up again. In the back of my mind lurked this fear that he would send the fire and brimstone I deserved. Fear is an effective tool in controlling people's behavior, but it also can be a powerful deterrent from the seeking of God. People don't invite in someone they are afraid of.

As my recovery progressed I still brought some of this fear of God with me. I was seeing more and more how great God's love for me really is, but I still wondered why there seemed to be so much fear in the Bible. Research of the word fear shows its use several times in the book of Proverbs.

> *"The fear of the Lord is the beginning of knowledge, but fools despise wisdom and discipline."*
> *(Proverbs 1:7 NIV)*

In the explanations at the bottom of the page in the NIV Study Bible it says, "Fear of the lord. A loving reverence for God." As Proverbs continues, it uses the word fear many times and continues to refer back to this explanation of the word fear. The American Heritage Dictionary defines the word reverence as "Profound awe and respect." This is a phrase that would always be attributable to God; in fact, the word profound isn't even strong enough. Perhaps intensely profound awe and respect is better. It may seem sort of silly that a man of forty-six years with an issue with the use of the word fear has never looked it up. The first definition of fear in the American Heritage dictionary is, "A feeling of agitation and anxiety caused by the presence or imminence of danger." This is what comes to mind when I hear the word fear, and it does not fit with the loving God I have come to know; my relationship with God is the farthest I can get away from imminent danger. He rescues me from the imminent danger of living a sin-filled life.

The second definition is, "A feeling of disquiet or apprehension." Over the years I have discovered that the only thing I can do to get away from disquiet and apprehension is to take it to God and ask Him to remove it, and He does, hence the phrase, "The peace that passes all understanding." Jesus said:

> *"I have told you these things, so that in me you may have peace. In this world you will have trouble. But take heart! I have overcome the world."*
> *(John 16:33 NIV)*

The fourth definition of fear is, "A reason of dread or apprehension." As Jesus said, in this world you will have trouble. Living in this world is the reason for dread and apprehension. Jesus is the cure for it, not the cause of it.

You will notice I skipped the third definition, but in all fairness to the accuracy of the Bible, I must share it. "Reverence or awe, as toward a deity." Now we have come back to the word reverence. I hope someday a scholar of the Bible will explain to me why the word fear is used so much in place of the word reverence. It makes no sense to me and causes confusion. I am however all right with not knowing all the answers, remembering that Jesus said we need to be able to accept Him with the simplicity of a child to get into heaven.

My struggle with the use of the word fear along with the hypocrisy of some of the dominant religious people of my childhood is a good example of having a good knowledge of the Bible coupled with a bad religious experience. One thing I've learned in recovery is that if it bothers me, it probably bothers others. Even though some of us think so, none of us are that unique. Of course, we are unique in many ways and no other person has exactly the same set of feelings and experiences as another; this is a matter of combination and order. There are no new feelings or problems; someone else has always been through it. There is always someone else struggling with the things we have struggled with. This has been demonstrated by countless numbers of people that have shared in twelve step meetings that they had a negative experience with religion in their past similar to mine.

As a member of the Christian church we need to acknowledge, try to understand and be empathetic of these types of issues when they come up in a conversation with someone with whom we want to share our witness. If we come back with a statement like, "You were wrong, you must have misunderstood," or, "That was certainly an isolated incident," we will quite likely just remind them of the negative experiences and reinforce their reluctance to come to church. Telling someone they are wrong is not the best method of winning them over. Our goal needs to be attracting them to church long enough for them to see that all Christians are not that way. When someone develops an idea on their own it is much more effective and lasting than having someone else's idea pushed on them. After a while they may want to discuss some misconceptions they have had about the church and that is the time to listen, make brief comments about their past so they know you heard them in a caring manor, and then help them see that the church has many positive aspects as well.

For some people the fear they have is because the Christian religion is largely unknown to them and we humans always tend to fear the unknown. Sometimes they can get up and running in a relationship with God quicker than a person that has had bad experiences with the church or people in it. They have, however, formed some sort of an opinion. Many people in the secular world think it is just hocus pocus stuff created as a crutch for the weak. They believe religion is the opiate of the masses. Whatever opinion they bring with them, it is important to realize they are going to be looking for what's wrong with church more than what is right. They will be sensitive to hypocrisy. Again, this is why it's important to look at yourself and see if you do indeed practice what you preach.

Perhaps the saddest reason of all that some people fear the church is that they are afraid of being rejected. They feel because of the lifestyle they have led, once people find out about their past and present life circumstances, they will be asked to leave. Yes, this does happen. I once had a friend that was a fellow recovering addict/alcoholic. He had recently been through a divorce and was quite sad about it. He thought his church would help him with it. Instead, the pastor approached him and said, "A lot of people in the church are taking your ex-wife's side. Perhaps it would be better if you find a new church." After telling this story, he looked at me in tears and said, "I have never been kicked out of a bar in my life." His opinion of the Christian church at that point was very low, and everyone he told the story to captured the same negative attitude about the church. Certainly the Christian church had not been helpful in his time of need.

At times people in the Christian church enter a debate on whether or not homosexuals and lesbians should be allowed in their church. This is a delicate issue because so many of us in the Christian church really can't comprehend what would cause a person to engage in this behavior in the first place. Some people worry that if they are allowed in, their children or others in the congregation will be influenced and become one of them. Yes, the Bible speaks out against homosexuality. It also speaks out against a whole host of other sins, many of which we as Christians are still guilty of. If the church is not for sinners–people that have made mistakes or been mislead–who is it for, perfect people? That sounds like a small congregation. When people outside of the church catch wind of such attitudes from within the church, they begin to wonder if their sin will exclude them from the church.

Many of us in the Christian church have been able to, through the grace of Jesus Christ, let go of much of our guilt. It is important to remember the people to whom you are witnessing are likely still carrying a full load of guilt and can be very easily made to feel so ashamed that they become certain the church can't or won't help them.

Another fear is that the church is going to try to influence them politically or tell them that there is only one possible way to worship God. Politics and religion are topics that can send someone packing quicker than anything. It is great that people in the Christian church care about what is happening politically and that they get involved in the political decision making process. It is also fine to belong to a certain denomination of religious affiliation, but leave it out of your witnessing. These are polarizing issues that can put tremendous distance between people in a hurry.

Ask yourself what is more important, to show them how smart you are because your have the right political view and belong to the only correct denomination of the Christian religion, or to reach out in love to this person that is suffering and is so greatly in need of Christ's healing power. My sponsor often asks, "Do you want to be right or do you want to be happy?" The need to push what we believe as the only right way is a serenity robber. It is also very unattractive. Most times just letting opinions of others that are in disagreement with yours go without a need to change them or prove them wrong will put you well on the road to peace and make you more attractive to those with whom you would witness.

Still others feel they won't fit in because the Christian church seems to be such a cliquey closed community. Sometimes we in the Christian church can't see the forest because of the trees. We start to focus so much on the needs of our congregation (the trees), we tend to forget about all those in need outside of our congregation (the forest). This "closedness" that develops is the direction a church filled with imperfect people often goes, unless the importance of constantly reaching out to the community is stressed. There is nothing wrong with fellowship with other believers, as a matter of fact, it is very important. But we can't let the importance of fellowship distract us from the equally important task of carrying the good news to everyone around us.

One of the best ways to check for perceptions people from outside the church may sense, is to try to look at your church from an outside perspective. Just like people need self examination to become more effective for God, so do churches. Start by asking what your church's mission is. Does it concentrate mainly on servicing the members that are already in attendance, or does it have a heart for reaching out to the community and welcoming anyone that is hurting in. If it doesn't seem to give importance to welcoming anyone that hurts, no matter what their sin is, it is always appropriate to ask your pastor or other elders in your church why not. Maybe it is as simple as focusing so much on who is there; they have lost sight of the suffering in the outside community. If this is the case, just pointing it out by asking may be enough to remind them to reach out more.

Maybe your church resists being out in the secular community and really does have a policy of not mixing with sinners. This is always sad and possibly indicates a misunderstanding of the basic message of Christ. Jesus specifically taught that we must not look down our noses on people plagued by sin and that we are to tell the good news to everyone, not just discuss it amongst ourselves.

> *"Jesus, undeterred, went right ahead and gave his charge: God authorized and commanded me to commission you: Go out and train everyone you meet, far and near, in this way of life."*
> *(Matthew 28:18–19 MES)*

> *"He told his next story to some who were complacently pleased with themselves over their moral performance and looked down their noses at the common people: Two men went up to the temple to pray, one a Pharisee, the other a tax man. The Pharisee posed and prayed like this: 'Oh God, I thank you that I am not like the other people–rob-*

*bers, crooks, adulterers, or heaven forbid, like this tax man. I fast twice a week and tithe on all my income.'*

*Meanwhile the tax man, slumped in the shadows, his face in his hands, not daring to look up, said, 'God, give mercy. Forgive me, a sinner.'*

*Jesus commented, 'This tax man, not the other, went home made right with God. If you walk around with your nose in the air, you're going to end up flat on your face, but if you're content to be simply yourself, you will become more than yourself.'"*
(Luke 18:9–14 MES)

Jesus spent a lot of time talking with and about the Pharisees because he wanted us to know how easy it is to fall in to the trap of self-righteousness. Our churches are not immune to this trap either, that is why it is so important to look at your own attitudes as well as your church's attitudes from time to time. This will insure that you are attracting the people that Christ wants us to reach, not scaring them away.

## 17. Feeling Judged

Perhaps the biggest way of insuring someone will not come to church with you, is making them feel like you are judging them. Because of our sin nature, we come by the practice of judging others in an effort to elevate ourselves naturally. We all have to make judgments all the time, for example, whether or not to get our hair cut and whether or not we want to go back to the same place we got our hair cut the last time. The negative sort of judgmentalism I am referring to is when we make judgments about others in a negative way to put them down, especially when accompanied by the attitude of, "At least I'm not that bad." None of us are perfect and all do this to some extent. It is however very important to be aware of and equally important, with God's help, to do less of it!

People that are caught up in painful, sinful behavior, already feel bad about what they have done. They don't need judgmental criticism from Christians to make them feel worse. Many people have found behaviors that help them stay in denial about their own pain. Examples would be all the addictive agents already referred to in chapter eleven. When they have a break in their armor and exhibit a moment of approachability, the last thing you want to do is pounce on them and drive home how horrible they are. This is the time for empathizing with their pain, and if the opportunity presents itself, to share some of the pain you have had in your life, so they don't feel alone. Then maybe you will have a chance to tell them about how Jesus rescued you from the pain of shame and quilt.

One of the worst things about judging people that are really hurting in this negative manner is that judgmentalism and compassion cannot coexist; they are mutually exclusive. Christ was always and is always compassionate. He cares greatly about the pain we feel because He experienced human pain firsthand. If anyone has the right to be judgmental it is Him, for in His time on this earth, He never sinned. Yet whenever someone came to Him in pain and suffering, instead of looking down His nose at them, He healed them. We are called by Christ's example to be compassionate toward those who still suffer.

If we as Christians are judgmental, it could of course mean we need to look closer at ourselves. Are we using the judgmental criticism of others as a way of ignoring our own sin? It is an easy trap to fall into, and the Bible warns us of the consequences:

> *"Those people are on a dark spiral downward. But if you think that leaves you on the high ground where you can point your fingers at others, think again. Every time you criticize someone, you condemn yourself. It takes one to know one. Judgmental criticism of others is a well known way of escaping detection of your own crimes*

*and misdemeanors. But God isn't so easily diverted. He sees right through all such smoke screens and holds you to what you've done."*

*(Romans 2:1–2 MES)*

Many people in the Christian church seem to think it is their job to point out sin. A speaker on one of the more popular Christian radio shows said, "The first job of the church is to be tough on sin, the second job is to reach out to the people sin has hurt." The second thought is great; it is the job of each and every Christian in the church, individually and as a group, to reach out to those in need of healing from the ravages of sin. However, the first job that he suggested sounds quite judgmental. This is a common attitude on Christian radio shows, one that gives Christianity a bad name. These people speak as if they have no sin, or at least their sin isn't as bad as that of nonbelievers. Even when they qualify their judgments by admitting to being sinners themselves, they still come across as though they think they are in some way better. They seem to enjoy condemning others. This is not the example Jesus set for us.

*"The religious scholars and Pharisees led in a woman who had been caught in the act of adultery. They stood her in plain sight of everyone and said, 'Teacher, this woman was caught red-handed in the act of adultery. Moses, in the Law, gives orders to stone*

*such persons. What do you say?' They were trying to trap him into saying something incriminating so they could bring charges against him.*

*Jesus bent down and wrote with His finger in the dirt. They kept at Him, badgering Him. He straightened up and said, 'The sinless among you go first: Throw the stone.' Bending down again He wrote some more in the dirt.*

*Hearing that, they walked away, one after another, beginning with the oldest. The woman was left alone. Jesus stood up and spoke to her. 'Woman, where are they? Does no one condemn you?'*

*'No one master.'*

*'Neither do I,' said Jesus. 'Go on your way. From now on don't sin.'"*

*(John 8:3–11 MES)*

It is not our job to throw stones at sinners. In most bad relationships between people, one or both of the people involved have the habit of taking the other person's sin inventory. Often, they do this in an effort to take the focus off of themselves. This is never helpful in healing a relationship, but many faltering relationships do heal if the people involved can start taking their own inventory and leave the other person's inventory to them. It is amazing how this one shift in attitude can have such a positive effect on a relationship between two people.

The purpose of the law is not to cut down and criticize others. The purpose is to show us how much we need the saving grace of God. We cannot save ourselves; no matter how hard we try we will always sin and therefore fall short of the glory of God.

> *"Its purpose was to make obvious to everyone that we are, in ourselves, out of right relationship with God, and therefore to show us the futility of devising some religious system for getting by our own efforts what we can only get by waiting in faith for God to complete his promise. For if any kind of rule-keeping had power to create life in us, we would certainly have gotten it by this time."*
> (Galatians 3:21–22 MES)

Jesus spent a great deal of time talking about the Pharisees and their attention to the details of the law. He did this because he knew it would be a pitfall for all of us. He also knew it is very unattractive behavior and would not be helpful in spreading the good news of the gospel to people that were hurting and needed the healing power of God. The interesting thing is, when people judge others according to the law put forth in the Bible, they are breaking the law. It is this hypocrisy that is so unattractive to the people we are called to witness to.

> *"Humble yourselves before the lord*

*and he will lift you up.*

*Brothers do not slander one another. Anyone who speaks against his brother or judges him speaks against the law and judges it. When you judge the law you are not keeping it, but sitting in judgment on it. There is only one law giver and judge, the one who is able to save and destroy. But you–who are you to judge your neighbor."*
*(James 4:10–12 NIV)*

Judging others is one of the worst forms of false pride and keeps us away from the humility that Christ modeled and the Bible teaches. Many people with addictive behavior have to battle pride and have talked about humility very often. It is a common topic for a twelve step meeting. If you are witnessing to a person with some twelve step background, they will have some idea of the importance of humility in a proper spiritual life. If you, as a witness for Christ, do not exhibit some humility, they will not be attracted to Christ; they will know something is not right.

Humility is not a bad thing. It is not a sign of weakness and it does not mean we let people walk on us like a door mat. Actually, humility is a tremendous source of strength. What it really means is that we know our own power is very limited and that God's power is unlimited. It is a matter of knowing our place in relation to God. It also means we know our place in relation to other people in that we are all sinners and basically in the same boat. Once we know our place, we can stop looking within ourselves or to other people for the solutions to life's problems and look to God instead. By looking to God we will gain peace along with all the other fruits of the spirit and as a result become attractive to people that have no peace and therefore become better witnesses for Christ. There is no shortage of passages in the Bible about humility. The following proverb is a commonly quoted one.

> *"First pride, then the crash–the bigger the ego the harder the fall.*
> *It's better to live humbly among the poor than live it up among the rich and famous."*
> *(Proverbs 16:18–19 MES)*

Listening to Christian radio is part of what keeps me motivated in getting out this message of compassion without harsh judgment and the message that even if you don't mean to judge, you can very easily sound judgmental to those who still suffer. The judgmental sounding attitude of many of these Christian speakers and their apparent lack of understanding of addiction, encourage me to speak out. The problem I have in doing so is that I wonder if I am guilty of the very thing I am accusing them of. Am I being judgmental of them by being overly critical of their behavior? I have struggled with this a lot and then it came to me: the only people that Christ was continually critical of were the religious leaders of the day. Perhaps there is a loophole here through which criticism of religious leaders becomes somewhat acceptable. I do struggle with the sin of needing to be right as much as anyone and I pray God will remove this defect of character or at least be able to make use of me in spite of this form of false pride.

Another speaker I recently heard on Christian radio was talking about how horrible the attitude of tolerance is. He shared about how he used to be a second class Christian in that he had accepted Christ, but didn't really strive to follow him. Now he considered himself a first class Christian because he had the willingness to stand up for what he believed in. Granted, there is a movement in secular society that believes everyone makes their own truth. That whatever someone decides is right for them is indeed right for them. Certainly this school of thought is often in disagreement with the Bible. Using this as an excuse to teach Christians an attitude of intolerance is also against the Bible. Were it not for the fact that God Himself has a tolerance for us sinners, we would all be in huge trouble. We don't have to approve of sin to be tolerant of sinners. We all need to take up our cross and follow Christ. The following is the passage on which the speaker was basing his boldness about telling others how horrible their behavior is.

> "Calling the crowd to join his disciples he said, 'Anyone who intends to come with me has to let me lead. You're not in the

> *drivers seat, I am. Don't run from suffering, embrace it. Follow me and I'll show you how. Self-help is no help at all. Self-sacrifice is the way, my way, to saving yourself, your true self. What good would it do to get everything you want and lose you, the real you? What could you ever trade your soul for?*
>
> *If anyone of you are embarrassed over me and the way I'm leading you when you get around your fickle and unfocused friends, know that you will be an even greater embarrassment to the son of man when he arrives in all the splendor of God, his father, with an army of holy angels.'"*
> *(Mark 8:34–38 MES)*

Granted, Jesus cautioned us about being embarrassed in relation to following him and his ways. The thing is, as we have already established, being judgmental is not one of his ways.

Another conversation heard on Christian radio recently was also using this passage as fodder for their exchange. A well-known Christian speaker was remarking in a negative way about how he thought it was politically correct to speak of God, but that it was not all right to speak of Jesus Christ. In his condemnation of the politically correct crowd, he wondered why people seem to be ashamed to be associated with Jesus. This caused me to think deeply, for I have fallen into this category. It has at times been difficult for me to speak of Jesus, yet easy for me to speak of God. I had to honestly ask myself if I was ashamed to be associated with Jesus, yet how could I be when I believe with all my heart that Jesus is my savior and that no other teachings in the history of humankind are as important as His. The answer saddened me greatly. I was not ashamed to be associated with Christ at all; I was ashamed to be associated with Christianity because of the horribly judgmental, inflexible, narrow-minded and intolerant attitude portrayed by so many Christians.

The person that was wondering about this was one of the very people I was ashamed to be associated with. The ironic thing is, I believe this person loves Christ greatly, has the best of intentions and has dedicated his entire life to the service of God. The problem is that he has been immersed in this environment for so long, he has difficulty putting himself in the shoes of those who still suffer and therefore doesn't realize how harshly he comes across to them.

The first speaker about tolerance went on to say how tolerance is such a bad thing among Christians and that it is responsible for "watering down the law." Actually, tolerance is a very important quality to have in a Christian that is witnessing to sick and hurting people. You will see all sorts of sin and perversion when consorting with the lost in an effort to win them over to Christ. This does not mean you think that sin is not sin or that sin is all right; it means that because you are dealing with humans you expect sin. If you can't tolerate sin, it is hard to be tolerant of the sinner. The sinner who still suffers is the very person God has asked us to reach out to.

We must always be on our guard to be sure we are not making a person feel as if we are judging them or their behavior. The time will come when they begin to look at their lives and will recognize their sin for what it is. At that time it is very appropriate to discuss the concept of sin and its harmful consequences with them, but if you start right off with shaking your finger in their face, telling them how awful their behavior is, you will lose many of them and even make it more difficult for other Christians to reach them in the future. Paul said that tolerance is one of God's attributes.

> *"So when you, a mere man, pass judgment on them and you do the same things, do you think you will escape God's judgment? Or do you show contempt for the riches of his kindness, tolerance and patience, not realizing that God's kindness leads you toward repentance."*
> (Romans 2:3–4 NIV)

This clearly says it is God's kindness, including his tolerance and patience that leads men to repentance. If we are to follow Christ as previously discussed, this is how we must behave. Christians that are harsh, criticizing and impatient with sinners don't attract, they repel.

An all important tool in witnessing to those

who still suffer is to not be shocked by sin. Don't be shocked by sin! Sin is all around us and yes, many times it is extremely shocking. If you are easily shocked by sin to the point where it is outwardly obvious to others, maybe you need to practice the appearance of not being so shocked. This is important because many of the people to whom you would witness already believe they could never fit in to a Christian congregation because of the shocking things they have done. If you react in a way that demonstrates how shocked you are, you will reinforce their attitude of not belonging when what you really want is to help them see they do belong.

Some Christians like to use scare tactics in their attempts to witness and with some people this works. We must, however, remain concerned about the people this tactic doesn't work with. How often do we hear a preacher threatening people with hell? It seems to make sense that people would be concerned about an eternity in hell and thus turn from their sin and repent. This may be true for some people that have their present needs met, but when a person is struggling so bad in the present that they are not sure they can go on, they don't think about eternity, all they know is they are already in hell on earth. That's right, many people are already in so much pain, they can't imagine it could be worse. If they think about an afterlife at all, they are convinced it cannot be as bad as the hell they are presently in. When people in this situation are approached with the "You're going to Hell" angle, they are apt to look at this person and think, "What could this person possibly know about hell?" Our immediate Christian witness needs to be aimed at getting them out of hell now, not at getting them out of some hell down the road they don't even have the ability at this time to contemplate. This does not mean the message about eternity is not extremely important, it just means that it may not always be the best thing to lead off with in your witnessing. Once someone has some of their present burdens lifted, they will become more able to consider eternity.

It is obvious that the Bible contains many commands, many points of law. As mentioned, they are there to point to our need for God's help. When Christians get hung up on quoting law, priding themselves on their knowledge of the law, and telling others they don't understand the law and love to argue the points of law with others, they certainly are not attractive and they also do not follow God's ways by doing so.

> *"I want you to put your foot down. Take a firm stand on these matters so that those who have put their trust in God will concentrate on the essentials that are good for everyone. Stay away from mindless, pointless quarreling over genealogies and the fine print in the law code. That gets you nowhere. Warn a quarrelsome person once or twice, but then be done with him. It is obvious that such a person is out of line, rebellious against God. By persisting in divisive-*

*ness he cuts himself off."*

*(Titus 3:8–11 MES)*

It is human nature to do these things. We all have a sinful nature whether we are Christians or not. It is easy to get caught up in being prideful about our knowledge of the law. This is why Jesus and the apostles spend so much time warning against being judgmental. The real message of the law is that God is willing to do for us what we cannot do for ourselves: pay our debt for our inability to keep the law. Salvation is a gift. When we see clearly that we are incapable of saving ourselves and realize that God has stepped in and sent Jesus to save us because we can't save ourselves, we become grateful and find compassion for those who still suffer. Compassion and gratitude are very attractive to others. The false pride of judgmentalism is extremely unattractive.

*"It wasn't so long ago that we ourselves were stupid and stubborn, dupes of sin, ordered every which way by our glands, going around with a chip on our shoulder, hated and hating back. But when God, our kind and loving savior God, stepped in, he saved us from all that. It was all his doing; we had nothing to do with it. He gave us a good bath, and we came out of it new people, washed inside and out by the Holy Spirit. Our savior Jesus poured out new life so generously. God's gift has restored our*

*relationship with him and given us back our lives. And there's more life to come–an eternity of life! You can count on this."*
*(Titus 3:3–8 MES)*

Thank you God for saving me from the ravages of sin and for the opportunity to witness to those who still suffer of your unending grace!

# 18. Is Our Absolute Truth Theirs?

Christianity and the Bible are synonymous. Christians consider the Bible to be the inerrant, absolute and complete word of God. Many Christians think it is the only source for information on how to live life. Because of this, it is no surprise that when two avid Christians are discussing almost any topic, they are soon quoting scripture and interpreting it in a way that backs up their supposition. This is as it should be. The Bible is God's instruction manual given to us so we know how to live. A good acronym for the word "Bible" is "*B*asic *I*nstructions *B*efore *L*eaving *E*arth." The Bible is what we base our Christian life on.

The Bible is the perfect word of God. In spite of this, it is important to realize that our human interpretation of it is not perfect, because we are not perfect. In fact, Satan is himself a scholar of the Bible and loves to twist its meaning and use it in a way that becomes a productive tool in keeping people from a deeply meaningful and useful relationship with God. Certainly we, as Christians, need to study, discuss and teach the Bible, but we need to do it with the realization that our interpretation could be wrong or at least taken out of context as it often is. In this light, the Bible is a very good reference when speaking to fellow Christians.

The important point here is to realize that when

you are discussing the problems and trials of this world with people that are not actively studying the Bible, your Biblically based argument backed up with Bible quotations will not necessarily be received as "absolute truth." The answer to the question, "Is our absolute truth theirs," is no. When we as Christians refuse to see this point and continue to throw out Bible quote after quote as if the Bible is as meaningful to everyone as it is to us, we can look like lunatics to the very people we are trying to convince of the fact that the Christian life is the most peaceful and sane way of life available.

A good illustration of this concept is my own personal experience. I hesitate to share it because it not only involves me; it involves my mother and brother. Before going on, I feel the need to issue the following disclaimer. Since the time of this incident my relationship with my brother and my mother are the closest they have ever been. I hold no grudges and have long since forgiven the hurt I felt. I have nothing but the deepest respect for the Christian life my mother and brother have both actively pursued for most of their lives. I dearly love both of them and my intent is not to hurt or punish them by publicly telling the story. My intent is to show others how they can get so caught up in their use of the Bible in proving a point, that they actually use the Bible as a tool to hurt another human being, something I am positive God never meant it to be used for.

A few years back, when I was at the deepest depths of depression and panic disorder imaginable, before God gave me the miracle medicine that has so much improved my illness, I lived in an old mobile home on my parents' property. Several years before that I had made the decision to give up my home in another city and move back to the farm I grew up on to help my mother care for my disabled father. He had reached a point of needing constant supervision and care. I knew my mother would push herself to do it so hard that it would very likely damage her health and to her, a nursing home was not an option. I moved back home because caring for my father was too big of a job for her on her own.

It had always been my childhood dream to live on and farm the land I grew up on, yet in the years previous to moving back home, I had made peace with the fact that in all probability it would never happen and came to the point where I had accepted the very real possibility of the farm being sold off to a stranger. When I came home I had no intentions of farming or owning the farm. At the time I was one year sober and all I knew was that God was clearly urging me to move home and help.

After living in the upstairs of my parents' house for a year, just looking at the empty farm buildings and watching the renters' farm the land; I bought some sheep and started to take back a portion of the farm from the renters. A year after that I bought an old mobile home and placed it across the yard from my parents' house. My farming activities increased and I found myself actually living my childhood dream. God is very good and truly gave me more than I expected.

The old home I was in had very dark walls and décor. Even though I appreciated having a place to call home, the dark décor did not agree with my depression. I decided to replace it with a new manufactured home that was much brighter and open feeling, thinking it would be good for my depressive mood. When I approached my banker about a loan, he pointed out how far I was getting in on land I didn't own and suggested it was time to look at the issue of land ownership. He was right; if I were to stay there and continue helping, steps needed to be taken to make it my permanent and legal home. My mother understood how I felt and we reached an agreement on a transfer of a portion of the land to me.

I always believed this to be appropriate. Even though keeping the land in my family was not my motivation for giving several years of my life to help care for my father, my being there had kept him out of a nursing home, the cost of which would have easily used up the entire value of the property. I certainly did not feel I was taking advantage of anyone. I always thought I was a tremendous help, a help beyond monetary value.

Once my mother and I had a firm agreement about what would be transferred and how it was to be transferred, I started spending money on a survey and attorney, then made financial commitments to the home manufacturer and firmed up my agreement with the bank. After everything was in the works, my brother showed up and talked my mother in to backing out on the deal we had reached. I was shocked. I knew people went back on their word and backed out of deals all the time, but not my mother. I was in disbelief. I told her that if we could not make this my permanent home, I would need to start putting my energy and money in my own property somewhere. She desperately wanted me to stay, but at the same time thought she should listen to the counsel of my older brother.

It wasn't long until I realized that my brother's motive for talking my mother out of our deal was that he considered me to be a fraud. He thought I was faking my illness in order to bilk the government out of his hard earned tax money in the form of disability payments. Now he figured I was moving on to defraud my mother of anything I could get my hands on. I do understand my illness is not visible to others, especially to those that know little about mental illness, but once my family knew about the diagnosis of doctors and psychologists, I thought I would at least have their support while going through the darkest, most difficult time in my life. I was absolutely crushed by my brother's accusations.

That evening as we sat in my mother's living room, trying to discuss the subject at hand, my brother sat across from me with a Bible in his hand. He would say something about how horrible it was to take advantage of an old woman and flip to some verse he thought backed up his argument and read it while violently striking the page of the open Bible with his index finger. He refused to listen to any reasonable or logical discussion and absolutely refused to see that he could be wrong. He just sat their flipping to verse after verse, pounding on them with his finger as he angrily read them.

He finally said he would accept my mother's decision, whatever that would be, but made it very clear that he was right because he could back up what he was thinking with the Bible. I told him again and again to make a logical argument instead of continually referring to the Bible, but he would not put it down. I wondered if he might actually break his finger as he struck the pages.

At that time, I was somewhat angry with God because I thought after all I had been through with drug addiction and divorce, plus the disagreements I had with my father, adding panic disorder and depression to the list was cruel and unfair. I had always considered the Bible to be the word of God but at that time was not engaged in any in-depth study of it. My brother's use of the Bible only increased my anger toward God. It had always been my understanding that the purpose of the Bible was to help people see their need for God's healing grace and to show us how to form the kind of loving relationship required to achieve said healing. I was quite certain the Bible spoke out against hurting others, yet here was my supposedly Christian brother using the Bible as the head of the spear he was continually jabbing me with.

In the end, my mother honored our original agreement and my brother never brought it up again.

I do understand that mental illness is difficult to comprehend and also how my brother was blinded by feeling a need to protect my mother. It sure would have been nice though if my brother could have put down his Bible long enough to listen to what the doctors and other mental health professionals in my life were saying. Maybe if he had not been so single minded about the Bible, he could have gained understanding of the situation from other sources and because of that understanding, been better able to model the compassion and empathy the Bible so ardently endorses.

The point is, because I was not in the most receptive frame of mind about the Bible at that time, because I had not yet completely worked through the acceptance of my mental illness and to some extend was still blaming God for it, my brother's choice to base his argument solely on Bible quotations made matters worse and was actually very hurtful to me.

This is an extreme example, yet many times when Christians continue to insert Bible quotations into a conversation, it begins to appear that they are not even listening to the other person. The insertion of Bible quotations means very little to the other person and because of this does not even seem to apply. Some Christians pride themselves on their knowledge of the Bible. Knowing what the Bible says is a very good thing when it comes to witnessing to those who still suffer, but how you use the knowledge can make or break a conversation about God. It is important to have a good understanding of the Bible so you can talk about the message of the Bible without quoting the Bible. In other words, learn to talk about the message of the Bible in every day language and, more importantly, learn the Bible so you can model the behavior it advocates. Christians not only need to practice what they preach if they want to reach others, they need to be able to practice without a lot of preaching. Remember, if our life does not appear to be attractive, we will not attract others to Christ.

After the 2004 elections, much was made of the red states and blue states. People from the secular side of life just couldn't understand what these evangelical Christians were all about. Actually, this is no surprise. If a person has had little exposure to Christianity or has had exposure, but has not based their life on it, evangelical Christians do seem a little different. If we believe as Christians that it is our job to reach out and witness to the secular masses, it is important to know they don't understand where we are coming from. Because of this, it is important for us to put ourselves in their shoes and think about how we must come across to those that don't actively follow the teachings of the Bible. It is our job to attempt to understand them because Christ commanded us to take the message of the gospel to all people, and we can't reach an audience we don't understand. This seems difficult to a person that has had a close relationship with Christ for a long time. Christians sometimes forget that Christ is filling a big void in their life. Everyone has this void that only God can fill, but when a person doesn't realize this, they attempt to fill it with anything they can find. When secular society is looked at in this light, they begin to become easier to understand.

The first thing to realize is that evangelical Christians speak a different language. There are many words commonly used in the church that simply don't get used in everyday secular conversation. Some examples are saved, born again, righteous, holy, redemption, repent, exalted, convicted of sin, sanctified, inerrant truth, etc. When Christian missionaries go to far off countries, they attempt to learn the native language so they can communicate, they don't sit and wait for the natives to learn theirs. So it is in our own back yard. If you want to communicate with your secular friends and acquaintances, you will have better luck if you don't speak a foreign language.

If you have studied your Bible enough, and pay attention to what words others are and are not using, you will be in a position to communicate the message of the Bible in a language they are more likely to grasp, or at least not in a way that turns them off because it sounds so strange. Be sure that a portion of your Bible study is dedicated to understanding the principles instead of just memorizing the words. People will learn about these words and concepts after they have been around the church awhile, but don't expect them to be readily accepted right off the bat. The use of a lot of this Christian jargon seems so foreign to many people that it tends to make them think you're some kind of religious nut and they just want to get away from you. A good example of how some of these phrases sound strange is found in the third chapter of John:

> "In reply Jesus said, 'I tell you the truth, no one can see the kingdom of God unless he is born again.'
> 'How can a man be born when he is old?' Nicodemus asked. 'Surely he can not enter a second time into his mother's womb to be born.'
> 'I tell you the truth; no one can enter the kingdom of God unless he is born of water and the spirit. Flesh gives birth to flesh, but the spirit gives birth to spirit. You should not be surprised at my saying, you must be born again. The wind blows where ever it pleases. You hear its sound, but you cannot tell where it comes from or where it is going. So it is with everyone born of the spirit.'
> 'How can this be?' Nicodemus asked."
> (John 3:5–9 NIV)

When Jesus told Nicodemus about being "born again," Nicodemus was confused by the use of such a strange term. Even after Jesus explained the concept, all Nicodemus could say was, "How could this be?" If a learned man like Nicodemus was confused by this terminology straight from the mouth of Jesus, do you think it will be any less confusing coming from your mouth to the ears of the average guy on the street? The concept that Jesus was referring to is tremendously important, one that all Christians eventually need to have some understanding of. The point is, don't expect people to grasp the concept right away. You can expect confusion over the use of such words and phrases. In that light, do you really need to start off with such words, or is better to find a way to introduce the concepts with words the person to whom you are witnessing is less likely to be confused over. Remember that Jesus used this phrase well into a conversation with a religious scholar; they were not the first words out of his mouth with the average guy on the street.

Christians often speak of ideal situations. They talk about how a good, healthy Christian family interacts with one another. They talk about how Christian people are good stewards of money and save for the future, pay all their bills on time and tithe. They speak of people with loving and caring attitudes toward one another. These are ideal situations, yet when they are talked about a lot without recognizing that they are the exception and not the rule in the human condition, people that are far from these ideal situations feel left out, like they have missed the bus, like there is no hope. Sometimes, it is very difficult for someone that has had such a poor experience in life to hear about nothing but the ideal Christian life. Again, this can be a circumstance that reinforces the attitude of not belonging when what you really want is to get them to see that they do belong. If you are talking about ideals, say they are ideals and that you understand that most people are far from them. It would even be nice if you could share a part of your own life that is far from the Christian ideal. Then the person is more apt to feel they belong. Later, you can start to share that it is possible for them, with the help of God, to move closer to such ideals.

Often, our reaction to the miracles God has performed in our own lives is to shout from the mountain tops about the glorious way God came to us, but it is essential to understand that this is not always the best approach in witnessing to those who still suffer. Bill Wilson fell into this trap soon after his conversion experience and it took someone else to point it out to him. In his first six months of constantly trying to pass his message of God-centered sobriety to others, he had succeeded with no one. He was counting solely on a religious approach and forgot about using other sources as well. He needed to put himself back in the shoes he had so recently been in and speak their language and speak to them in a way that got their attention. The following quote illustrates this concept.

> "After a few months I saw the trouble was mainly in me. I had become very aggressive, very cocksure. I talked a lot about my sudden spiritual experience, as though it was something very special. I had been playing the double role of teacher and preacher. In my exhortations, I had forgotten all about the

medical side of our malady, and the need for deflation at depth so emphasized by William James had been neglected. We weren't using the medical sledgehammer that Dr. Silkworth had so providentially given us.

Finally, one day, Dr, Silkworth took me back down to my right size. Said he, 'Bill, why don't you quit talking about that bright light experience of yours; it sounds too crazy. Though I'm convinced that nothing but better morals will make alcoholics really well, I do think you have the cart before the horse. The point is that alcoholics won't buy all this moral exhortation until they convince themselves they must. If I were you, I would go after them on a medical basis first.'" (The Language of the Heart, page 199)

The Bible is a wonderful gift that God has given us. It is a very important tool in reaching others for Christ, but it is not the only tool God gave us to use and oftentimes it is not the first tool to pull out. Sometimes you have to help people see the need for God in their life before they are receptive to the Bible, and often this process does not happen over night.

## 19. Effective Help is Ongoing Help.

Oftentimes the thought of reaching out to the less fortunate among us conjures up images of some big crusade or tent revival, or perhaps a special speaker at our church that stirs the crowd and finishes with a dramatic alter call in which many new believers come forward. There is nothing wrong with this–it's always great to see new people come to the Lord–but it's equally as important to realize most people need a lot of help, support and guidance and that the first time dedicating or re-dedicating their life to Christ is only a beginning. Oftentimes Christians, while comparing their life here on earth to the time spent in eternity, use illustrations like, "This life is but one dot on the line of eternity," or, "This life is just one grain of sand on the beach of eternity." So it is with comparing that moment of giving one's life to Christ with the rest of the time here in this life.

Many people have been so hurt that they have difficulty trusting anyone or anything. They have built a protective wall around themselves and don't really let anyone in or anything out. This is an awfully lonely and sad existence, and of course we want to bring people out of this shell into the glorious presence of God. We need to realize that this can take a long time, quite possibly the rest of their lives. They will make progress a little at a time. It is always tempting to rush this process along by pushing our own version of the law and ideals on them, thinking they could almost immediately be at the point in their walk with the Lord that we are. But this will only make them frustrated and sound so foreign and difficult to them, that they will think this Christian life is too hard and give up. Instead, they just need our love, the love that God has so freely given us, and they need it over a long time, remembering that love is patient and kind. Perhaps the most comprehensive definition of love is contained in first Corinthians.

> *"Love is patient, love is kind. It does not envy, it does not boast, it is not proud. It is not rude, it is not self-seeking, it is not easily angered, it keeps no record of wrongs. Love does not delight in evil but rejoices with the truth. It always protects, always trusts, always hopes, always perseveres."*
> *(1 Corinthians 13:4–7 NIV)*

Notice this passage ends with hope and perseverance. We must never lose hope for someone that is struggling and never give up. As for trying to speed spiritual growth up in a person by constantly quoting the law to them, don't do it. Pushing the law on others is not how we keep the law; loving others is how the Bible says we fulfill the law.

> *"Don't run up debts except for the huge dept of love you owe each other. When you*

*love others, you complete what the law has been after all along. The law code–don't sleep with another person's spouse, don't take someone's life, don't take what isn't yours, don't always be wanting what you don't have, and any other "don't" you can think of–finally adds up to this: Love other people as well as you do yourself. You can't go wrong when you love others. When you add up everything in the law code, the sum total is love."*

*(Romans 13: 8–10 MES)*

Being a Christian is a journey, not an event. A starting point is important because a journey can't start without the first step. It is exciting to be involved in the kind of evangelism that sees, on a regular basis, a large harvest of souls for the lord. However, the bulk of help that those who suffer need is far less glamorous, but it is what the Bible calls us to do. We are to form relationships with these new believers and do whatever we can to help them along. It is not our job to force a lot of rules and regulations on them; it is our job to love them and to continue loving them. Many people have never felt much real love. Nothing has more power to heal than sharing the love we get from God with others. We are to accept them with open arms.

*"Welcome with open arms fellow believers that don't see things the way you*

*do. And don't jump all over them every time they do or say something you don't agree with–even when it seems they are strong on opinions but weak in the faith department. Remember, they have their own history to deal with. Treat them gently."*
*(Romans 14:1 MES)*

It is so important to remember that we have not experienced the same history that they have. They may well have been through some horrors that are unimaginable to us. We need to treat them gently, with patience, always remembering that they did not get to the state of suffering they are currently in overnight. Many of those who still suffer carry with them years and years of scars. It took along time to accumulate the hurt and mistrust, and it may take a long time to heal from it.

One thing that will help us to be more understanding is to remember the phrase, "But for the grace of God go I." It is so easy to fall into the trap of thinking "If only they would have made the choices I've made, they wouldn't be in this mess. Therefore, if I push my choices on them they will get better." Remember, you did not choose what circumstance you were born into. For all you know, you would have not handled their circumstance even as well as they did. If you are reading this, you were born into a circumstance that a large percentage of the world's population was not born into–at least you can read. We tend to compare ourselves to those in the society around us and forget how privileged most of us are. When we realize that we didn't have everything to do with how "great" we have become, that we could have just as easily been born into families where poverty or horrible abuse was the norm, families with no concept of God, it becomes easier to have patience and compassion for those who were born into less than adequate situations. The best way to keep this attitude in our witnessing is to give thanks to God, everyday, for all the rich blessings He has bestowed on us.

Another thought that can keep us from being the kind of boastful and proud that the Bible says love is not, is to be aware of the fact that at any minute we could lose the financial situation or health that have been so generously given us. If you don't believe this consider the stock market crash of 1929 or think about the person in your community struck down by cancer in the prime of their life. Being in the position to reach out to others in loving, patient, un-forceful kindness is a great blessing.

Having the love to give others is a great gift, one that will go stale if we do not continually share it. A glass of water can only hold so much and it will not stay fresh for long, but the pipe bringing the water to the glass can over time contain a tremendous amount of water, always fresh water. If we are a container of God's love, we fill up and God's love becomes stale. If we are a conduit of God's love through which God's love travels on its way to others, we will have a never-ending fresh supply. The strength God gives us is not to build ourselves up, it is to help others.

> *"Those of us who are strong and able in the faith need to step in and lend a hand to those who falter, and not just do what is convenient for us. Each one of us needs to look after the good of those around us, asking ourselves 'how can I help?'*
>
> *That's exactly what Jesus did. He didn't make it easy for himself by avoiding people's trouble, but waded right in and helped out. 'I took on the troubles of the troubled,' is the way scripture puts it. Even if it is written in scripture long ago, you can be sure it is written for us."*
>
> *(Romans 15:1–4 MES)*

This is what we are here for–to help others. Those who still suffer need daily support and encouragement. They need to be nurtured in the development of their relationship with Christ. They may need help in many aspects of their life, but be sure you are not doing something for them they should be doing for themselves. Try to teach them to fish, instead of giving them a fish. Help them develop their own set of moral guidelines instead of imposing yours on them. Always remember how important your example is in this process.

It can be difficult in our busy lives to do much giving to others. It is easy to walk up to someone new in the church, shake their hand and say, "Welcome, it's

## Effective Help is Ongoing Help

so nice to have you here, I hope you'll come back." It takes much more loving self-sacrifice to walk up to a new person and ask, "Is there anything I can do to help? Do you need someone to talk to? How can I help make you feel more welcome?" And then follow through with such offers for help, maybe for a long time to come; fully knowing they will never be able to pay you back. It may help if you don't lose sight of the fact that maybe someday they will do the same for someone else that is in need.

This may be an area in which Christian churches could take a cue from twelve step groups. Consider the following quote from the "Big Book" of Alcoholics Anonymous and ask yourself if you would be willing to do these things, if God asked you to.

> "Never avoid these responsibilities, but be sure you are doing the right thing if you assume them. Helping others is the foundation stone of your recovery. A kindly act once and a while isn't enough. You have to be a Good Samaritan every day if need be. It may mean the loss of many nights sleep, great interference with your pleasures, interruptions to your business. It may mean sharing your money and your home, counseling frantic wives and relatives, innumerable trips to police courts, sanitariums, hospitals, jails and asylums. Your wife may sometimes say she is neglected. A drunk may smash the furniture in your home or burn

a mattress. You may have to fight with him if he is violent. Sometimes you will have to call a doctor and administer sedatives under his direction. Another time you may have to send for the police or an ambulance. Occasionally you will have to meet such conditions." (Alcoholics Anonymous, page 97)

The lifestyle of loving others as long as they need loving is not necessarily easy, and often other people will not understand why you do it, but Christ will greatly reward you for it, in this life and the next. Remember that Jesus wants us to wade right in and help out those who still suffer.

## 20. Will We Always Make a Difference?

Wouldn't it be nice if we could just tell someone once how unnecessary much of their pain is and have them come immediately to God, turning their problems over to him and getting a fresh start? This is not reality. Many people will never come to Christ; they will take other paths. Nowhere in the Bible does it say we will be able to reach everyone. In fact, experience says we will fail to reach many.

> *"For as I have often told you before and now say again even with tears, many live as enemies of the cross of Christ. Their destiny is destruction, their god is their stomach, and their glory is in their shame. Their mind is on earthly things."*
> *(Philippians 3:18–19 NIV)*

The truth is God gave us a free will, the choice of what we do with it is ours. This is a gift that we can do whatever we please with. As we already know, self-centeredness is a big part of the human condition. Humans want what they want and they want it now. Ironically, the one thing God asks of us, if we want His help, is that we choose to turn the illusion of control we have back over to Him. Jesus says we must ask, seek and knock, if we want the healing miracle of God in our lives.

> *"Ask and it will be given to you; seek and you will find; knock and the door will be opened to you. For everyone who asks receives; he who seeks finds; and to him who knocks, the door will be opened."*
> *(Matthew 7:7–8 NIV)*

I use the term illusion of control because none of us really have control; if we did, we would be God. God could at any time force us to do anything He wanted us to do. There are also countless other forces over which we have no control as well, such as weather and natural disasters, car accidents or illness. In spite of this, humans often think they do have control, but it is an illusion. The reason God gave us this illusion was simply to see what we would do with it. After all, if God simply forced us to come to him, it wouldn't mean much. God wants us to ask for his help of our own free will. Many people are so attached to the illusion of control, that they simply cannot bring themselves to the point of giving that control up.

I had an interesting conversation with my psychiatrist recently. Of course I have no way of knowing where he stands with God and it is never my job to make that judgment of someone, however, it would appear that he is a highly educated man without a lot of room in his life for God. In spite of this, he has been a tremendous help to me and I have no doubt that God has used him as a tool in my recovery and I am very grateful for the effort he has invested in me as a patient. God brought me to him and other mental health professionals because over a long period of time, I have attempted to turn control of my life over to the care of God.

When I first started to see my psychiatrist, he held out little hope for my recovery. He would have considered it a great success if I was simply able to do my own shopping without leaving my half filled shopping cart sitting in the middle of the store and going to my car without buying anything because I was too panicked to stand in the checkout line. I would have been happy with this amount of progress as well, but God has granted me recovery far beyond this. My psychiatrist has been very surprised by how far I have come and has said I could be a poster child for recovery from panic disorder. He does not understand what has caused this recovery, and when I refer to God he says "Oh, you mean that God thing." He neither condemns nor supports God, but in his defense I have to say he has been very supportive of my twelve step involvement.

The last time I saw him he went on and on about how well I was doing at taking control of my life back. He pointed out several areas in my life that were out of control in the past, areas that in his assessment I now clearly do have control over. His assessment is, however, incorrect. In the past when I tried to be in control of these aspects in my life, they were hopelessly out of control. Over time, as I have turned more and more control of my life over to the care of God, I have gotten better. The source of the miracle recovery I have experienced is God. I have given up more and more control of my life to Him. The irony here is that the more control I give up, the more control I appear to be taking back in the eyes of my psychiatrist. People have a hard time believing that it is a good thing to give up control; this world places a huge value on being in control, not on giving up control.

One of the reasons many people will never receive God is that they cannot get far enough past their self-pride to ask for help. This not only applies to many highly educated and successful people, it applies to many down and out people as well. They often believe, because of low self-esteem, that they do not deserve help. This belief of not deserving help is a form of self-pride. Thinking they are so different that even if others do deserve help, they don't deserve help, is a form of pride that keeps them from asking, seeking and knocking.

There are also many cases of individuals that do ask for help and things seem to be going in the right direction when all of the sudden, they have fallen back into their old damaging behavior and appear to have once again turned their back on God. This is commonly referred to as relapse and is a very common occurrence in addiction recovery. People in twelve step groups often say they are back on the research committee to find out if their life really is a disaster without God, and inevitably they find out it is. A lot of these people, after many more hard knocks, do come back to God, but some never do. The Bible backs up the fact that this will occur.

> *"The spirit makes it clear that as time goes on, some are going to give up the faith and chase after demonic illusions put forth by professional liars."*
> (1 Timothy 4:1 MES)

It is normal to wonder why someone who has clearly asked for help all of the sudden no longer appears to be receiving help. Perhaps this is best explained in the "Big Book" of AA when it says:

> "We are not cured of alcoholism. What we really have is a daily reprieve contingent on the maintenance of our spiritual condition. Every day is a day when we must carry the vision of God's will into all of our activities." (Alcoholics Anonymous, page 85)

The answer to the question, "Why did they stop receiving?" may be as simple as, "They stopped asking." But perhaps there are more reasons less easy to understand. I once had a friend in a twelve step group whom I had actually prayed with and I was certain this person was very sincere in their request for help from God. Even though this person clearly had a longing for peace, she would soon be drunk again. After a while I lost touch, but heard reports from time to time of someone seeing her when she appeared to be drunk. One day I heard that she was drunk and had been taken to the hospital with blunt trauma to the head. Shortly after her arrival she was pronounced dead. This is a hard situation to understand and I have had to realize it's all right if I don't always understand, but I have often wondered if God knew she would never be able to have the peace she had asked for in this world and since she was saved, God simply decided to take her on to the next world where she could have peace.

Oftentimes, people do have a better go of it the second or forty second time around. Isn't it wonderful that we serve a God of second chances? I also have a friend that went through drug and alcohol treatment nine times and spent a good share of his life in jail. Society said he was hopeless, yet today, by the grace of God, he has been sober for many years and devotes a good deal of his time to helping others. It was fun to share with him the moment in his late forties when he had to renew his driver's license. It was the first time in his life he held a driver's license long enough for it to expire on its own and therefore needed to be renewed.

It can seem futile when many people don't seem to be getting the message of love you so much want to convey, but again, we are not responsible for the results, just the effort. People in twelve step groups often share how something someone said or did long before they began turning their life over to the care of God had stayed with them and was instrumental to their finally seeking the loving care of God. Many times the person that said or did this thing never knew they had an effect on this person. Recognition is not the goal in this type of sharing. People that reach out to those who still suffer realize the value of planting seeds. They cannot know which seed will grow and which seed will not. They just know that if they plant enough, God will cause some of them to grow.

We know we can't reach everyone, but everyone we do reach is something to rejoice over. We must never lose hope!

> *"Or imagine a woman who has ten coins and loses one. Won't she light a lamp and scour the house, looking in every nook and cranny until she finds it? And when she finds it you can be sure she'll call her friends and neighbors: "Celebrate with me! I have found my lost coin!" Count on it–that's the kind of party God's angels throw every time one lost soul turns to God."*
> *(Luke 15:8–10 MES)*

## 21. We Love Who God Puts in Front of Us.

As much as we want to, we don't get to pick who gets better and who doesn't get better. If it were up to me, I would have everyone get better, I would want no one to suffer, but it's not up to me. I would not do a good job as God, because I am not capable of understanding the intricacies of the universe. In the movie "Bruce Almighty," Bruce complains about God's choices and is given the chance to take over for God. It's not long before he is overwhelmed by prayer requests. He can't imagine really listening to all of them, so he decides to just answer them all yes. As you could imagine, the result was at best chaotic. One example went something like this: 200,000 people won the lottery, but each of them only won $2.37. If I were God, it would be a mess.

Maybe you wouldn't make that big of a mess; you only want to pick a few of your close friends and family members to get better. No one could blame you for that. But this is not the case. Many of us see someone we love in great agony and want so very much to rescue them. As we discussed before, if they don't ask to get better, they won't. One of the big drawbacks of getting hung up on wanting a certain person to get better is that you may end up putting a lot of effort toward a person that God has not yet made ready and miss directing God's mercy to another. God chooses who he wants us to help.

> *"For he says to Moses, 'I will have mercy on whom I will have mercy, and I will have compassion on whom I have compassion.' It does not therefore depend on man's desire or effort, but on God's mercy. For the scripture says to Pharaoh: 'I raised you up for this very purpose, that I might display my power in you and that my name might be proclaimed in all the earth.' Therefore, God has mercy on whom he wants to have mercy, and he hardens whom he wants to harden."*
>
> *(Romans 9:16 NIV)*

God always has a reason for doing what he does, saving who he saves and hardening who he hardens. Who are we to question God? If we are to have peace, we need to trust that God is working toward a higher purpose that we cannot comprehend and simply love who he puts in front of us.

I have a friend and neighbor that I would have liked to see get sober years ago. We sat together on the bus since the first grade. We smoked pot for the first time together. We partied together many times. After I moved away, he was the only one I stayed in touch with. When I came back to visit my parents, I would visit him. When he saw me coming he would roll a joint and have it ready to light as soon as I walked up to him. We had a similar upbringing in that our parents were religious and we both had a childhood belief in God. He was one of the only people I discussed God with while smoking pot.

When I finally, by the grace of God, was able to quit drugs and alcohol, I stopped going to see him because I was afraid of how I would handle his offer to smoke a joint. Many times I thought of him and from time to time would hear how much trouble he was in with his drug use. I wanted so badly to help him, but never saw God opening a door to do so. Eventually I did go see him and offered to take him to an AA meeting. We talked awhile but he declined. I have since heard he is doing much better and that God once again plays an important role in his life, but God didn't use me to bring it about. I don't know why God chose another avenue, I just know he did and I accept that and am glad to hear the news that my friend's life is going better.

I have however had the privilege of being part of the recovery of the person I had my first drink with. It is always such a neat thing to sit together in a recovery meeting and share with people that he gave me my first drink and I took him to his first AA meeting. I don't know why God decided to make me part of this person's recovery and not a part of the other, but I rejoice along with the angels for the progress made in both their lives.

Sometimes we object to the people God puts in front of us. They may be of a financial or physical stature that turns us off. They may be uneducated and difficult to communicate with. They may be dirty and smelly. It is a very human thing to shy away from people that bother us in some way. When it happens the best solution is to pray continually for God to give us the power and desire to love whom ever he puts in front of us. Sometimes we have to pray for the ability to love our enemies and sometimes we have to pray for the ability to love the unlovable.

We can always know, if we are willing to seek God's will instead of our own, he will choose to make us part of someone's recovery and I promise you will never tire of being part of the miracle of recovery in someone's life, no matter who that someone may be. We see God in the faces of those who still suffer, especially the ones God has chosen to put right in front of us.

## 22. Why do Bad Things Happen to Good People?

Sometimes we just don't want to be around people that suffer. It is hard to comprehend and deal with all the pain and suffering in this world. Sometimes we ask, "If God is so good, why do so many people suffer?" The Bible tells us that pain and suffering are a part of the human existence because of disobedience to God. Paul tells us:

> *"For the wages of sin is death, but the gift of God is eternal life in Christ Jesus our Lord."*
> *(Romans 6:23 NIV)*

From this we can see that pain and suffering are the result of our behavior–it is what we have coming. Because God is so good, he found a way to help us escape some of the pain and suffering by sending his son to take our place, but it will not take full effect in this world. We don't have to get very far into the Bible before it lays out the consequences of our disobedience to God. The first chapter tells of the creation of the world, the second tells of the creation of man and by the third chapter, man is already in trouble; pain and suffering have entered the world. God had warned man of the consequences of certain behaviors.

## *12 Steps*
## To a More Effective Christian Witness

> *"But you must not eat from the tree of knowledge of good and evil, for when you eat of it you will surely die."*
> *(Genesis 2:17 NIV)*

This is the way the universe was set up. If man were to follow the instructions God gave him, suffering could be avoided, but there was another force that wanted to see man suffer, a source of evil that would challenge every guideline God set forth. He was and is the great deceiver and has been successful all along at turning man against God. Of course this is the force we call "Satan" or "the Devil."

> *"The woman said to the serpent, 'We may eat fruit from the trees in the garden, but God did say, You must not eat fruit from the tree in the middle of the garden, and you must not touch it, or you will surely die.*
> *'You will not surely die,' the serpent said to the woman. 'For God knows that when you eat of it your eyes will be opened, and you will be like God, Knowing good and evil.'"*
> *(Genesis 3:2–5 NIV)*

Satan knows our every weakness; he knew we couldn't avoid the temptation of wanting to be like God. The idea that any human being could be like God was a lie and continues to be a lie, but many of us fall for it everyday by trying to run our own lives instead of turning them over to God. From that first time of disobedience, the consequences have been laid out.

> *"The very ground is cursed because of you; getting food from the ground will be as painful as having babies is for your wife; you'll be working in pain all your life long. The ground will sprout thorns and weeds, you'll get your food the hard way, planting and tilling and harvesting, sweating in the fields from dawn to dusk, until you return to the ground yourself, dead and buried; you started out as dirt, and you'll end up dirt."*
> *(Genesis 3:17–19 MES)*

Pain, suffering and death have been a part of this world since the dawn of man. God warned us about it, but we listened to Satan and as a result suffering came into the world. God didn't have to do anything about it–He didn't cause it, man and Satan caused it. But God in his goodness offers us a way out and of course that way out is the good news of the gospel of Jesus Christ.

This world always has been and always will be filled with pain, suffering and death. By accepting this truth we are able to work with people who still suffer without becoming overwhelmingly disappointed when people still suffer.

"Burnout" is a commonly discussed phenomenon in the recovery community. It refers to people that have dedicated themselves to helping people deal with addiction, suddenly not being able to do it any more. They have gotten their hopes up for someone one too many times and they just can't bear to see another failure. This is always sad because it often happens to some of the most caring and talented people recovery has to offer. People in the Christian church can burnout as well when they have too many disappointments in their attempts to witness to those who still suffer. The only way to avoid this is by accepting up front that we live in a fallen world and many of those we witness to will not understand what we are trying to say and those who do will still have some pain and suffering.

It can seem at times that our efforts are completely worthless, but it helps to know that every time we are witnesses for Christ, whether there is visible growth in the people we witness to or not, there is tremendous growth in us. Remember that the most selfish thing we can do is to become selfless and giving to others. The road to peace and the path out of this fallen world will pass by many of those who still suffer. Every time we share a bit of God's love with them, we store up treasures in heaven.

The most important concept about being able to work with others is that of acceptance. We need to accept this sinful world as it is, not as we would have it. One of the personal stories in the back of the "Big Book" of Alcoholics Anonymous sums it up best when it says:

"And acceptance is the answer to all my problems today. When I am disturbed, it is because I find some person, place, thing or situation–some fact of my life–unacceptable to me, and I can find no serenity until I accept that person, place, thing, or situation as being exactly the way it is supposed to be at this moment. Nothing, absolutely nothing, happens in God's world by mistake. Until I could accept my alcoholism, I could not stay sober; unless I accept life completely on life's terms, I cannot be happy. I need to concentrate not so much on what needs to be changed in the world as on what needs to be changed in me and my attitudes.

Shakespeare said, 'All the world's a stage, and all the men and women merely players.' He forgot to mention that I was the chief critic. I was always able to see the flaw in every person, every situation. And I was always glad to point it out, because I knew you wanted perfection, just as I did. A.A. and acceptance have taught me that there is a bit of good in the worst of us and a bit of bad in the best of us; that we are all children of God and we each have the right to be here. When I complain about me or about you, I am complaining about God's handiwork. I am saying that I know better than God." (Alcoholics Anonymous, fourth edition, page 417)

*12 Steps*
To a More Effective Christian Witness

You will never be more alive, than when you accept this world as it is, seek the will of the one who created you, and spread the healing love of Jesus Christ to those who still suffer!

# Epilogue

It has been several months since the actual writing of this book, and as an end note just before production I would like to make a couple of updates. First I wanted to pass on the reaction I received from my letter to Rick Warren that was presented in the first chapter. When I sent it, I sent it twice. One copy went to the main church office at Saddleback and the other to the Celebrate Recovery office. As of today the "Letter from Pastor Rick" that contains so much misinformation about twelve step groups remains unchanged. One month after sending the original copies of the letter, a staff person from Rick Warren's office did respond with the following letter:

Dear Alvin,
    Thanks for writing. Pastor Rick reads all his e-mail and regrets that he isn't able to respond to each one personally as he would love to.
    It's obvious that you have a real passion for recovery. Pastor Rick will appreciate that you trusted him enough to share your heart. With your permission I will forward your e-mail to our Celebrate Recovery Team and ask them to respond to you directly.
    May God continue to guide you as you seek Him and lead others to sobriety and to a relationship with Christ.

*12 Steps*
To a More Effective Christian Witness

All God's best to you,
MaryAnn Webb
Correspondence Coordinator
Saddleback Church
Office of the Pastor

---

From this letter I assumed that Pastor Rick had been made aware of my letter. I also assumed that even though the Celebrate Recovery office didn't bother to respond to the letter when I originally sent it to them, they would surely now respond when it came from Pastor Warren's office. They never did.

Several months past and I heard nothing further. As I finished writing this book I realized how busy they are at Saddleback and how easy it would be to over look a letter such as the one I sent them, so I decided to contact them again. I spoke directly to an office staff person in Pastor Warren's office and told them I had included the letter in this book and thought it only fair to give them one more chance to respond and she suggested I re-e-mail it to the person who had originally responded and that she would tell her of the importance of the matter. This conversation produced the following letter from me:

---

Dear Maryann Webb:
A few months ago I sent a rather lengthy letter to pastor Warren in response to his "message by Pastor Rick" found on the Celebrate Recovery web-

site. In it I outlined some obvious misunderstandings he holds concerning twelve step groups such as Alcoholics Anonymous. My main apprehension about it is that when someone from a twelve step background has been pointed toward God in a secular twelve step group and is looking toward a relationship with Christ as their understanding of God, runs across this misrepresentation of the twelve step community, they may actually be pushed further away from Christ.

Often times when people are already skeptical of the Christian church and they see such blatant misrepresentations of the truth by a prominent church figure, they think they were right all along, that the Christian church is just a bunch of self-righteous hypocrites. Why Pastor Warren continues to alienate such a large group of people that are genuinely searching for a relationship with God eludes me. You responded briefly a month after I sent this letter and indicated in your response Pastor Warren had or would read it. From his lack of response and the fact that there is no change in his message on the Celebrate Recovery website, I conclude that this matter is of little significance to him.

The reason that I am bringing this issue to your attention one more time is that I have written a book entitled "Twelve Steps to a more Effective Christian Witness" that is currently in production with Tate Publishing and will soon need to write an epilogue if I am going to do so. In this book I included a copy of my letter to Pastor Warren because it is such

*12 Steps*
To a More Effective Christian Witness

a good representation of the misunderstanding many in the Christian community hold about the twelve step community. In the epilogue I hoped to have a positive response from Pastor Warren to report, but if I only have a lack of response from him that is what I will write about.

I spoke with someone else in your office on the phone today and she suggested I send a reply to this e-mail back to you since you had originally responded to me. If you want to bring the Celebrate Recovery people in on this feel free to do so, but they have never responded to any of my e-mails in the past, I did send them a copy of my original letter and it went unanswered. Quite frankly this letter was to Pastor Warren and it is his response that I would be most interested in. I know he is a devoted servant of God with a large ministry to oversee, but I do believe this is a matter important enough for his attention.

Please respond soon, the time I have to write an epilogue is running out. Thank you so much for your attention to this matter. You will find your original response and my original letter if you scroll down.
Alvin Velsvaag

---

Here is the response to my last letter:

---

Dear Alvin,
Thanks for writing back. I apologize for any miscommunication in my previous e-mail. I was ask-

ing for your permission to forward your original e-mail to our Celebrate Recovery Team. When I didn't hear back from you I assumed that you did not want me to pursue that avenue and I did not forward your e-mail. I felt that you were sharing trusted information with Pastor Rick and I shouldn't forward it without your awareness. Now that I have your approval, I'm forwarding this e-mail to our Celebrate Team and asking someone to connect with you as soon as possible.

This is an exciting time for Saddleback Church and at the same time quite demanding. We've just celebrated our 25th Anniversary and we are moving full steam ahead into Pastor Rick's vision and God's plans for the next 25 years!! Next week, Pastor Rick will be hosting the annual Purpose Driven Church Conference for pastors. Then, he will be traveling extensively from June through August. He's also devoting much of his time in preparation for the launch of the Global P.E.A.c.e. Plan which will be introduced in the fall.

Along with all of the excitement there are a lot of demands on Pastor Rick's time. As such, we are limiting his commitments and carefully scheduling his time. I know Pastor Rick's heart and he would love to review your material, however, he's even saying "no" to many of his longtime friends right now in order to focus his efforts on this next season of ministry. So Pastor Rick appreciates your grace in understanding why he is unable to connect with you personally and he wishes you all the best with a suc-

cessful launch of your book.
    Blessings,
MaryAnn
MaryAnn Webb
Correspondence Coordinator
Office of the Pastor

---

From this letter I get the message that the twelve step community, representing millions of people who are seeking God to alleviate their problems, is of little importance to Pastor Warren. He is simply too busy to re-address an issue that he has already publicly commented on, even though his original comments are in error and could actually be hurting many people. His misinformation could keep them from Christ, because that misrepresentation seems hypocritical and is therefore unattractive.

I have still to this day had no response from the Celebrate Recovery office. It would seem as though my comments are even less important to them, at least Pastor Warren's staff made a response.

The other issue I wish to address here is my current twelve step commitment. As you have gathered, I was involved with Celebrate Recovery at my local church, but as time went on I became more and more disillusioned with them. My main concern was their seaming disregard for AA and other secular twelve step groups. They appear to want to replace them instead of supplementing them. I believe this is a poor approach because it is not building a bridge between the Christian community and the twelve step community. When it got to the point where I realized that I could not recommend Celebrate Recovery to anyone in the twelve step community, it became clear I needed to end my involvement with it. This left me disappointed because I so much wanted my Church to have a Christian twelve step ministry.

While searching the web, I ran across an organization called "Overcomers Outreach" or "OO" for short. Their web address is www.overcomersoutreach.org/. They have a very informative website. Their number one goal is to build a bridge between the Christian church and the twelve step community; they whole heartedly support groups like AA. They even recommend that people involved in OO remain involved in groups such as AA; after all, what a great opportunity to witness for Christ among people that are searching for God. Of course they respect AA's traditions and do not recommend evangelizing during meetings, but do realize the immense opportunity to witness for Christ before and after meetings. I am amazed at how similar their thinking is to mine and am now happily involved in an Overcomes Outreach ministry at my Church.

I knew God would show me where to serve if only I would ask. Last night our OO meeting topic was the "will of God." I do believe my involvement with OO is the will of God for me and that I will continue, as the eleventh step suggests, "Praying only for knowledge of His will for us and the power to carry that out." My hope is that you will do the same.

# Bibliography

*Alcoholics Anonymous.* New York, NY: Alcoholics Anonymous World Services, INC. 2001

Baker, John, *Celebrate recovery; Stepping Out of Denial into God's Grace.* Grand Rapids MI: Zondervan. 1998

Hemfelt, Dr. Robert and Dr. Richard Fowler. *Serenity a Companion for Twelve Step Recovery.* Atlanta, GA: Thomas Nelson, Inc. 1990

*Pass It On, the Story of Bill Wilson and how the AA Message Reached the World.* New York, NY: Alcoholics Anonymous World Services, Inc. 1984

*The American Heritage Dictionary.* New York, NY: Bantam Doubleday Dell Publishing Group, Inc. 1992

*The Language of the Heart.* New York, NY: The AA Grapevine, Inc. 2002

*Twelve Steps and Twelve Traditions.* New York NY: Alcoholics Anonymous World Services, Inc. 1996

Warren, Rick *The Purpose Driven Life.* Grand Rapids, MI: Zondervan. 2002

Contact Alvin Velsvaag
or order more copies of this book at

TATE PUBLISHING, LLC

127 East Trade Center Terrace
Mustang, Oklahoma 73064

(888) 361 - 9473

Tate Publishing, LLC

www.tatepublishing.com